EUROPE'S HIDDEN CAPITAL MARKETS

Europe's Hidden Capital Markets

Evolution, Architecture and Regulation of the European Bond Market

JEAN-PIERRE CASEY

KAREL LANNOO

CENTRE FOR EUROPEAN POLICY STUDIES
BRUSSELS

The Centre for European Policy Studies (CEPS) is an independent policy research institute based in Brussels. Its mission is to produce sound analytical research leading to constructive solutions to the challenges facing Europe today.

The views expressed in this report are those of the authors writing in a personal capacity and do not necessarily reflect those of CEPS or any other institution with which the authors are associated.

CONTENTS

List of Figures

List of Tables

List of Boxes

ACKNOWLEDGEMENTS

The authors are grateful to their CEPS colleague Camille Selosse for her competent research assistance. They also acknowledge with gratitude comments on the draft report made by numerous participants who attended a CEPS workshop on bond markets held in Brussels on 17 May 2005. David Self from the former International Securities Market Association (ISMA) – now ICMA (International Capital Market Association) – must be thanked for providing data on the international bond market and for his assistance in familiarising the authors with the dataset. Likewise for Antoine Weber (Luxembourg Stock Exchange), Marco Angheben (European Securitisation Forum) and Jean-Michel Six and Gerben De Noord (Standard & Poor's) for sharing S&P research outputs.

Discussions with, and comments from Marco Laganá (European Central Bank), David Clark (European Investment Bank), Donald Ricketts (Fleishman Hillard), David Lawton and Tim Rowe (UK Financial Services Authority), Garry Jones and Duncan Wales (ICAP), Richard Britton (ICMA), Michael Ridley (JP Morgan) and Manfred Schepers, Bertrand Huet, Micah Green and Michael Decker (The Bond Market Association) were very instructive and are gratefully acknowledged.

This study was made possible by funding from the ISMA, but the views expressed are those of the authors alone and do not represent those of ISMA, CEPS or any other institution with which they are associated. The authors accept full responsibility for any errors or omissions.

EXECUTIVE SUMMARY

Non-equity financial markets used to be 'hidden' in Europe, in the sense that relative to their size, they received less attention from ordinary investors and the media than equity markets. Given that bond markets play a crucial role in the economy through the capital allocation process, monetary policy decisions and the hedging of risk, not to mention their immense size, this situation was somewhat puzzling, but it has been changing. Nevertheless, since the overwhelming majority of bond trading is still conducted off-exchange, there remains a certain generalised misapprehension among investors and regulators about how these markets operate. Therefore this report aims to demystify and elucidate European bond markets.

Chapter 1 highlights recent developments in European bond markets in light of the ongoing transformation of the European financial system triggered by financial sector liberalisation, the accelerated process of disintermediation and the introduction of the euro. The chapter provides numerous comparisons with the United States as a benchmark, looking at the respective value of outstanding debt securities issued in, and the growth rates of various bond market segments. Bond market microstructure and recent developments in the architecture of primary and secondary markets are examined in Chapter 2, especially in light of the evolving phenomenon of electronisation of fixed income trading. Recent regulatory measures taken at the level of the EU institutions that will impact on European bond markets are summarised in Chapter 3. Chapter 4 highlights critical aspects of the policy debate as the European Commission prepares to undertake its review of Art. 65.1 of the markets in financial instruments directive (MiFID). The latter mandates the Commission to explore the possibility of extending the pre- and post-trade transparency requirements prevailing under the new equities regime to non-equity markets. A final chapter presents a set of policy recommendations based on conclusions drawn from Chapter 4.

In the wake of accelerating disintermediation in EU financial markets and catalysed by the introduction of the euro, bond markets – and especially the corporate bond market – have grown at phenomenal rates, in some segments by over 500% in value terms since 1999. In sharp contrast with 1992, when the European bond market was nearly half as small as that in the US in terms of GDP, by 2005 they had almost fully converged. Debt securities issued in European capital markets are characterised today by longer maturities, significantly larger borrowing programmes and greater liquidity than they were a decade ago. Impressive rates of growth are also mirrored in the market for asset-backed securities, as the phenomenon of securitisation also gathers speed, which is part of the overall shift from relationship banking to arm's-length finance on the European continent. The explosive growth observed in the primary market was not lost on the secondary market, which also witnessed tremendous gains in trading volumes, greatly improving liquidity. Both the euro and increasing electronic trading are responsible for these developments.

The new legislative measures introduced as part of the Financial Services Action Plan (FSAP) to create a truly integrated capital market, although more onerous than the previous regime, should contribute to the further growth of capital markets in the EU. The prospectus directive accommodates different regimes and maintains a healthy degree of regulatory competition for bond issues. The International Accounting Standards 'roadmap to equivalence' agreement with the US will allow other jurisdictions to follow, avoiding a flight of the bond business to non-EU financial centres. Questions can nevertheless be raised about the new MiFID regime, which remains very burdensome for investment firms. Going forward, the main task for regulators and supervisors is to make the new regime work, through consistent implementation and enforcement. The initial evidence on these matters is not comforting, however.

In light of the forthcoming MiFID review, the issue of whether similar price transparency requirements should be applied to bond markets as to equity markets remains particularly contentious, because bond and equity markets are fundamentally different, in terms both of their structures and in the nature of their participants.

The fixed income business has long been a critical factor in the ongoing widening and deepening of European capital markets. A wide and growing variety of product choice has carefully been tailored to meet the demands of issuers and investors with diverse needs and has contributed in a major way to financial innovation in the EU. Nevertheless, the business potentially faces one of the greatest threats yet to its independence as a largely self-regulated market. The European Commission will soon review for the European Parliament and Council of Ministers whether to extend pre- and post-trade transparency requirements to bonds. Whether a disclosure framework for fixed income trades that closely resembles the existing one for equity shares under MiFID is desirable remains a hotly contested point. Because of the specificity of the fixed income business, namely, that it is quote-driven and liquidity providers risk their proprietary capital to make markets, it is vital that policy initiatives be attuned to the risks of imposing a top-down market infrastructure. Any ill-designed statutory measures that emerge at the European level could seriously undermine the dynamism and competitiveness of these markets.

In the wake of recent investor losses in fixed income investments and the growing retail participation in fixed income more generally, there can be no doubt that regulators' concerns about bolstering retail investor protection in this market segment are valid. However, it is important that such measures not focus solely on introducing statutory regulation affecting the microstructure of bond markets, but rather touch especially on the wider matrix of improving corporate governance, rooting out conflicts of interest in the advisory function and fostering financial literacy among investors. The all-important question in the regulatory debate will be to find ways, preferably through incentive schemes, and possibly through limited statutory regulation but only as a last resort, on how to concretely address these legitimate concerns about investor protection while ensuring that the proposed measures are the instruments that best address the source of the problem. Any proposed measures must also be able to achieve the desired results at a minimal cost, without engendering unintended spillover effects, such as inflicting damage on the liquidity-providing function.

In the debate on investor protection in equity markets, particular focus has been placed on best execution and reducing transaction costs. Because retail trades are frequent in equity markets, this regulatory strategy made sense. However, the retail presence in fixed income can be characterised by buy-and-hold type strategies and a wide-spread sense of false security regarding invested principal. As a result, regulators would be mistaken to focus their attention disproportionately on reducing transaction costs through equity-style best execution requirements. Much more important yet is the safeguarding of principal. This CEPS report highlights some possible strategies that regulators could employ to this effect, including the important question of giving impetus to market initiatives aimed at improving documentation standards and encouraging the channelling of retail investments in high-yield and complex structured products through investment funds.

If market efficiency is the ultimate objective driving regulatory interest in improving price transparency, one must ask whether greater transparency will enhance market liquidity. Neither the theoretical nor the empirical literature gives unambiguous indications that greater transparency would improve liquidity. This is all the more true of fixed income markets, since some bonds may be or become structurally illiquid; hence, policy initiatives will do little to improve their liquidity.

1. Trends in European Bond Markets

1.1 Development and integration of European bond markets

i. The shift away from relationship banking to arm's-length finance

Over the past two decades, the European financial system has been undergoing a deep transformation, evolving from what used to be a predominantly bank-based structure to greater reliance on vibrant capital markets as a source of funding and risk mitigation. The proximate causes driving the ongoing process of change were the nearly simultaneous internal and external forces, both political and economic, that weakened the power of vested interests staked in preserving the antiquated industrial structure of relationship finance prevalent in Europe until that time.[1]

First came the liberalisation in the 1980s of capital controls and deregulation of the banking sector within what then was the European Economic Community (EEC, which became the European Union in 1993). Already in the 1970s, following the collapse of the Bretton Woods system, the gradual trend towards liberalising the capital account was motivated by the recognition that shielding the independence of domestic monetary policy from global capital movements under a floating-rate system was redundant. Subsequently, partly as the logical corollary of relaxing capital controls within the EEC (reflecting policy initiatives ultimately aimed at achieving monetary union), and partly also due to the dominant influence of the neoclassical consensus on the benefits of competition, a wave of deregulation in the financial sector swept over Europe. As the EEC was laying the groundwork for monetary integration internally, capital movements worldwide increased greatly both in magnitude and scope as a

---

[1] For a detailed exposition of the political economy of vested interests stalling financial development in Europe for the better part of half a century, see Rajan & Zingales (2002).

result of the wider phenomenon of financial globalisation. Together, these internal and external forces amounted to important pro-competitive effects, which in turn improved the efficiency of financial services provision and fostered product innovation. The combination of internal liberalisation and financial globalisation also paved the way for greater volumes in trading that greatly enhanced the liquidity of the European capital market. But ultimately, it was the introduction of the euro occurring in the midst of this ongoing transformation that provided the most significant impetus to deeper integration and to the further development of European capital markets, magnifying the positive effects initially brought about by the aforementioned forces.

The reference point for any study of European financial markets must therefore be 1 January 1999, when the euro first emerged as a currency for wholesale transactions, because this date marks the conclusion of one of the most impressive examples of a policy-driven process aimed at overcoming market fragmentation.[2] From the earliest days of financial integration in the EU, it was recognised that achieving a single capital market within the EEC was inconceivable so long as no unified currency emerged (Richebächer, 1969). The introduction of the euro underpinned the development of truly pan-European financial markets, whereas in the past financial activity had mostly remained constrained within national boundaries and intermediated by banks. Bonds and their derivatives – the focus of the present study – were not left untouched by this seismic policy initiative. Once the cornerstone was in place, there resulted an explosion in cross-border issuing, investing and trading in fixed income (and other) securities. An important by-product was financial innovation. By expanding the opportunities to hedge risk on the supply side and to diversify portfolios on the demand side, new instruments will allow for more sophisticated risk mitigation techniques through interest rate-linked options and futures instruments and significantly, the huge growth in over-the-counter interest rate swaps; their introduction can lead to greater portfolio efficiency, increasing returns for a given level of risk.

---

[2] Although the initial inspiration for the creation of a single currency was political in nature (as suggested by the Werner report or the negotiations on the parities at which the national currencies would be fixed), the efficiency gains of surrendering national control over monetary policy were deemed to be sufficiently large as to warrant the creation of a single currency, widely seen as the missing cornerstone of the single financial market.

As private capital markets have gained in importance in Europe over the past two decades, bank financing has correspondingly diminished in scale and scope *relative to* arm's length financing (although in absolute terms, it has risen, reflecting financial deepening). This was certainly not the case 25 years ago. In 1980, relative to GDP, bank deposits in the EU were 60% larger in continental Europe than in the US or UK; the ratio of bank credit to GDP (measured as bank loans to the private sector) on the continent was twice that of the latter two countries in 1980 (Rajan & Zingales, 2002). Today, this large gap has narrowed considerably: in the year 2000, the same ratio was only 30% larger on the continent than the US/UK average.[3] This amounts to an extremely impressive rate of convergence, since 50% of the gap was closed in 20 years' time. Particularly interesting was the convergence in financial structures that occurred over the sample period between the UK and continental Europe. Financial structures have traditionally been rather disparate across the EU. But as a result of policy choices and market-driven outcomes, the convergence process underway has been gathering pace since the start of EMU. Murinde et al. (2004) analyse the pattern of corporate financing and test their hypothesis of financial system convergence across seven EU countries. Their results indicate that convergence has been occurring, with a pronounced – albeit gradual – shift to heavier reliance on retained earnings

---

[3] Upon closer examination of the figures, one must note – and the cited authors do not state it explicitly in their paper – that the gap narrowed *only* because bank deposits relative to GDP have exploded in the UK between 1980 and 2000, rising from 28% to 107%, showing a large increase in commercial bank intermediation. By contrast, over the same time period, bank deposits to GDP fell in the US from 54% to 38%. In other words, relative to the US, the importance of bank deposits in Europe actually *increased* between 1980 and 2000. While it was 120% in 1980, it reached 245% by the year 2000. Nevertheless, one must be careful not to immediately conclude that there has not been a profound transformation of the European financial system in recent years. These figures may also reflect the fact that US household savings have deteriorated demonstrably over the same time period, possibly explaining the lower deposit-GDP ratio for the US. Vis-à-vis the UK, however, the ratios have been converging between 1980 and 2000. The ratio was larger on the continent by 230% in 1980 and was actually surpassed by the UK by 2000. The point of this exercise is to demonstrate that the convergence between the UK and the continental European financial systems was the driving force behind the closing of the gap between the respective US-UK average and continental bank deposits to GDP ratios.

and greater direct recourse to market financing in the form of equity and bond issuance, leaving a lesser role for bank lending to play.

ii.   *International comparisons of debt, equity and bank loan finance*

Despite the ongoing transformation, European finance still remains largely dominated by bank intermediation, both in absolute terms and relative to the United States. The following international comparisons with Japan and the United States show that relative to equity finance, debt financing – and bank loans in particular – remains far more important in the EU (see Figure 1.1a). At the beginning of 2004, the value of bank assets relative to GDP was 237%, 73% and 146%, in the EU-15, the US and Japan, respectively.[4] By contrast, equity financing is more than twice as important in the US as it is in Europe (in relative terms), accounting for 116% of GDP in the US compared with 62% in Japan and 54% in the eurozone countries. In terms of market-based finance, bond markets are more important in the US (and Japan) at 169% of GDP, but the EU is not far behind, reaching 142% of GDP in 2003. Combining debt securities with bank lending, total debt finance in the EU is 379% of GDP, compared with 242% in the US and 315% in Japan.

Figure 1.1a Bond, equity and bank assets markets in EU-12, EU-15, US and Japan, end 2003 (% of GDP)

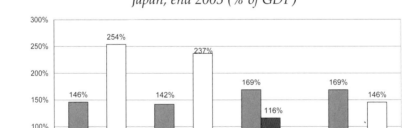

---

[4] It is interesting to note that if one looks only at eurozone countries, market-based finance is even smaller relative to GDP. This is no surprise, since the UK economy accounts for the significantly greater value of equity finance in the EU-15 than in the eurozone countries alone (64% of GDP compared with only 52%) and the lower value of bank assets relative to GDP (237% as opposed to 254%).

Figure 1.1b Bond, equity and bank assets markets in EU-12, EU-15, US and Japan, end 2003 (€ billions)

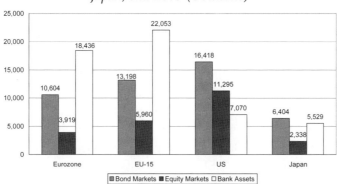

In value terms, the analysis is similar to the situation relative to GDP, since EU and US GDP are more or less equivalent. Total assets of European banks have grown significantly over the past decade, nearly doubling from about €11.8 trillion in 1995 to €22 trillion by January 2004 (Figure 1.1b). Because in 1995 the value of bank assets in the EU was roughly double that of debt securities (whose combined total then was €5.1 trillion), bond markets had a lot of ground to catch up. Slowly, they are gaining importance relative to bank lending, since, at €13.2 trillion (end-2003), the value of debt securities issued by EU firms and governments represented 62% of the total value of bank assets, whereas the same figure stood at below 50% in 1995. Coincidentally, they are also gaining in relation to the American bond market. In 1999, the total value of debt finance (capital market, not bank loans) in Europe amounted to €8 trillion; the corresponding figure for the US was €12.7 trillion. By end-2004, however, debt finance in Europe reached a value of €13.5 trillion, compared with €16.7 trillion for the US.

Of the three main sources of external finance – bank lending, bonds and publicly-traded equities – the last is the least important in the EU, with the total market capitalisation of EU exchanges in 2003 (€6 trillion) being slightly above a quarter of the value of bank assets. There was a point in 1999 when equity markets reached the same importance as bond markets, but that trend could not be sustained in the aftermath of the collapse of the tech bubble, which vanquished the new markets and triggered very significant, albeit gradual, declines on the major European exchanges. Private equity investment remains a minute fraction of total firm financing in the EU, although growth rates since 1990 have been very impressive (Figure 1.2). Net annual investment in 1989 totalled about €4 billion, compared with €30 billion in 2003. Over the past 15 years, according to the European Venture Capital Association, total investments in private equity in the EU rose from €14.8 billion to €140 billion.

Figure 1.2 Total EU private equity investment (€ billions)

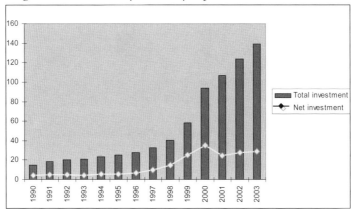

Note: Total investment measured at cost.

Source: Authors' own calculations and European Venture Capital Association (EVCA).

Due to a different set of initial conditions, a perpetuation of the gap in market-based finance between the EU and the US is inevitable, at least for the near future. Nevertheless, as disintermediation gains speed in Europe, the gap is slowly being closed. This is nowhere more evident than in the remarkable transatlantic convergence process that has occurred in bond market activity in recent years (see Figures 1.3a and 1.3b below).

Figure 1.3a Bond markets in EU-15, US and Japan, 1992-2003 (% of GDP)

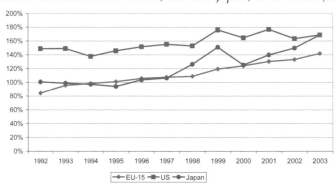

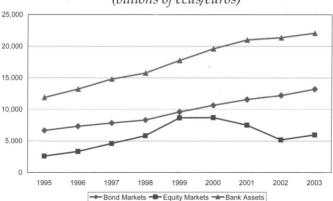

*Figure 1.3b Bond, equity and bank assets markets in EU-15, 1995-2003
(billions of ecus/euros)*

Whereas in 1992 the size of the European bond market stood at little more than half that of the American one relative to GDP (just over 80% compared to 150%, respectively), the faster growth of the former has meant that in fewer than 10 years, the initially large gap was virtually closed: today, the combined value of debt securities in the US reaches 170% of GDP, while the equivalent figure for the EU is roughly 140%. (Coincidentally, one can also observe a similar trend in Japanese capital markets.) As is the case for equities, the European bond market has been growing markedly faster than bank finance over the past decade, achieving a growth rate of 105% over the period 1995-2004. Corresponding figures for the value of bank lending are 86% over the period.

iii. International comparisons of bond market growth rates

Because the trend toward deeper financial market integration in Europe coincided with the wider trend of financial globalisation, it is difficult to determine the proximate cause of the explosive growth in debt issuance that occurred in Europe in the late 1990s and early in the 21st century. Analysing the counterfactual is one way to arrive at a conclusion: How much of that growth would have occurred in the absence of monetary union? In order to obtain a rough figure, we compare the growth rates of European bond markets with those of the US and Japan. The greater the difference between the respective growth rates, the greater is the probability that a good part of that difference can be accounted for by the 'single currency effect,' or specifically *European* financial market integration, as opposed to financial globalisation.

Since the advent of EMU, European bond markets, propelled by private debt issuance, have been growing very rapidly, much more rapidly even than those in the United States and Japan (Table 1.1). Overall, over the five-year period 1999-2004, the amount outstanding in debt securities issued by governments, corporations and financial institutions in the EU-15 grew by 65%, or some 35% faster than the rest of the world, which only achieved a growth rate of 50%. This significantly higher growth rate suggests that European integration spurred deeper capital market integration, above and beyond what would have been achieved by financial globalisation alone. The market for corporate debt securities provides just such an example. Whereas the American corporate bond market grew by 35% between 1999 and 2004, its European counterpart easily eclipsed it with an extraordinary growth rate of 283% over the same period.

Table 1.1 Total growth in amount outstanding of debt securities, 1999-2004

	Eurozone	EU-15	US*	Japan	Rest of world	World
Total debt securities	69%	68%	32%	55%	59%	49%
Government debt securities	50%	44%	7%	109%	66%	49%
Debt securities issued by financial institutions	77%	101%	60%	-21%	95%	65%
Corporate debt securities	283%	216%	35%	1%	56%	43%

* US figures were calculated in dollar, not euro terms, since exchange rate movements would significantly affect the ratios for the US and not reflect true market development.

Source: Authors' own calculations from BIS data..

Evidently, the introduction of the euro had a significant impact on the currency denomination of many international debt issues, as the greater liquidity of the currency and its widespread acceptance as a vehicle (reserve) currency along the lines of the US dollar has led to a great increase in the choice of the euro as a currency of issuer. Whereas in 1993 only 25% of international debt was denominated in currencies that today make up the euro, today the corresponding figure is around 40%. Figure 1.4 shows the consolidation in vehicle (reserve) currencies that has prevailed in the past 12 years. Currencies that once had a role in international finance, such as the Japanese yen, the Swiss franc and the Canadian dollar, have all but disappeared from the international debt market.

Figure 1.4 International debt issues by currency

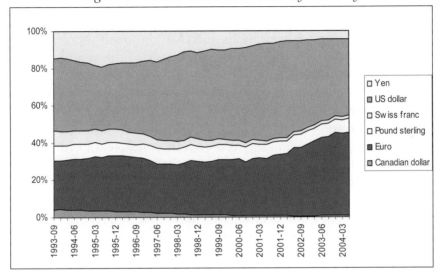

1.2 European bond market overview and trends

i. *International versus domestic debt securities in the EU*

Worldwide, domestic capital markets remain the dominant source of debt finance, although the international debt market has been growing far more rapidly.[5] In the past 25 years, the total value of domestic debt has trebled, whereas the international debt market grew by a factor of 17.[6] Growth in the volumes of the aggregate world domestic debt market was accounted

---

[5] "The BIS definition of international securities (as opposed to domestic securities) is based on three major characteristics of the securities: the location of the transaction, the currency of issuance and the residence of the issuer. International issues comprise all foreign currency issues by residents and non-residents in a given country and all domestic currency issues launched in the domestic market by non-residents. In addition, domestic currency issues launched in the domestic market by residents are also considered as international issues if they are specifically targeted at non-resident investors" (see BIS, 2003, pp. 13-14).

[6] Authors' own calculations from BIS data.

for primarily by the United States and Japan. Japanese domestic debt surged in the wake of the severe banking crisis that disrupted the Japanese economy for nearly the entirety of this period, the result of an aggressive Keynesian fiscal expansion to counter ineffective monetary policy and of the political decision to re-capitalise sinking banks. Mostly due to the declining state of public finances, as the Japanese debt-to-GDP ratio climbed from around 70% of GDP in 1990 to over 170% of GDP in 2003 (see IMF, 2004).[7]

Over the past 18 years, the growth rates in issuance of international debt easily were multiples of GDP growth in many countries, above and beyond EU borders, which implies that although the euro may have been an important determinant propelling growth within the EU, there were powerful external forces at work. Whereas the total value of international debt securities (all issuer types) was merely €608 billion[8] in 1987, it exceeds €9,800 billion today, a pace equivalent to a doubling in value every year. The world's three largest economies display very different characteristics in this category: Japan is still a very closed capital market, and perhaps due to the conglomerate structure of the keiretsu and the close ties that it fosters between corporates and their banks, in addition to the very high savings rate of households, Japanese firms have yet to develop a culture of tapping global capital markets. Less than 4% of Japanese debt is held overseas (see Pesek, 2005). At the same time, it is clear that in the EU, the growth of international debt securities in terms of value outstanding has been nothing short of phenomenal, particularly since the introduction of the euro (Table 1.2). Growth rates of international bonds have also been high in the US, which has traditionally been a largely autonomous and introspective capital market.

---

[7] Despite these already alarming figures, many analysts argue that this nominal figure understates the true state of Japanese public finances, as a number of contingent claims on Japanese government coffers are excluded from the figures. When the value of contingent liabilities are included, that is, of government guarantees to semi-public industries, Japanese public debt is said to exceed 200% of GDP.

[8] At current (June 2005) exchange rates.

Table 1.2 European bond market growth, 1999-2004

Country	International debt securities outstanding (€ billions)		Domestic debt securities outstanding (€ billions)		Growth rate, int'l debt	Growth rate, domestic debt
	1999/3	2004/12	1999/3	2004/12	1999-2004	1999-2004
Austria	55.4	120.5	120.1	174.1	117%	45%
Belgium	83.1	179.7	330.3	374.1	116%	13%
Denmark	18.9	32.4	250.4	356.2	71%	42%
Finland	31.7	53.6	75.2	95.1	69%	27%
France	178.1	552.4	1050.3	1645.4	210%	57%
Germany	433.2	1384.5	1677.3	1715.1	220%	2%
Greece	20.0	65.1	87.1	167.5	225%	92%
Ireland	20.5	90.1	26.5	69.7	340%	163%
Italy	85.9	405.3	1298.4	1827.8	372%	41%
Luxembourg	6.3	27.8	-	-	343%	-
Netherlands	154.4	409.9	303.6	517.8	166%	71%
Portugal	13.5	75.3	56.5	116.0	457%	105%
Spain	109.7	344.7	330.8	672.2	214%	103%
Sweden	75.4	103.4	217.1	240.2	37%	11%
UK	276.1	833.7	637.5	802.0	202%	26%
Eurozone	1192.0	3709.0	5356.1	7374.7	211%	38%
EU-15	1562.4	4678.5	6461.0	8773.2	199%	36%
US	755.4	1991.5	11944.4	14785.1	164%	24%
Japan	245.4	176.2	4264.4	6832.6	-28%	60%
World	3543.1	8262.0	24819.9	33943.7	133%	37%

Source: Authors' own calculations with BIS data.

Domestic debt markets in the EU continue to be dominated by government debt, both sovereign and sub-national. In only three countries in the sample of 15 in Figure 1.5a below do government issues not 'crowd out'[9] private issuance, namely, in Denmark, the Netherlands and United Kingdom. On the other hand, some countries' domestic debt markets

---

[9] 'Crowding out' of private borrowing by heavy government borrowing is defined (arbitrarily) by the authors as government debt not accounting for more than 50% of total value of domestic debt issues.

remain completely dominated by government debt, especially those in countries like Greece, Hungary and the Czech Republic, which have a tradition of less developed capital markets. It is no surprise that the United Kingdom has the most vibrant domestic corporate debt market in the EU, with a share of just less than one-third of the total value of domestic debt. Financial institutions represent the second largest share of domestic debt issues after government entities in all EU member states except Denmark, where they surpass official sector bonds in value terms.

Figure 1.5a Domestic debt securities, by sector composition

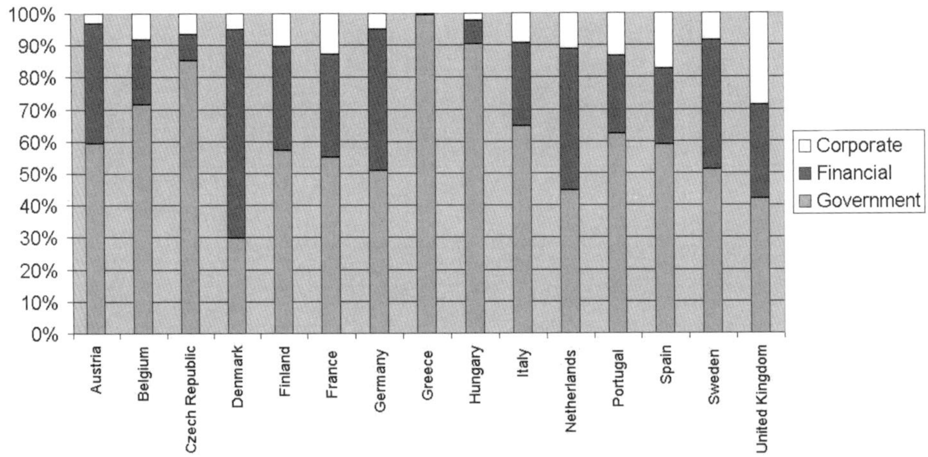

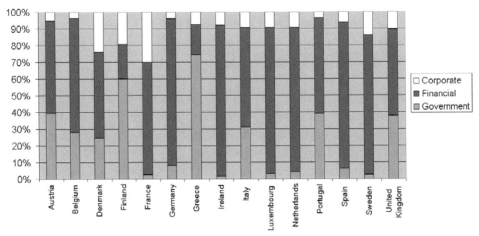

Figure 1.5b International debt securities, by sector composition

Source: Authors' own calculations with BIS data.

International debt issues are largely, and in some EU member states overwhelmingly, dominated by financial institution issues (Figure 1.5b). This result should come as no surprise, since financial institutions continue to be the main source of finance for European firms, and thereby engage in large-scale lending activities for which they must find sources of funding. Due to their expertise in, knowledge of, and experience with financial markets, banks and other financial intermediaries have a long experience of tapping international capital markets for funding purposes. As can be seen from the figure, international debt issues by Finnish and Greek entities continue to be dominated by government activity, countering the general tendency in the EU.

Interestingly, the EU (defined as European governments, corporations and financial institutions) accounts for the majority of the international capital market in value terms, capturing a market share of over 50% (Figure 1.6a, last column). The source of this domination may be proximity to the London-based international bond market as well as a mixture of legal, tax and accounting reasons. But it is also due to heavy issuance by European governments and financial institutions, which could not be met by demand from domestic investors alone. Each accounts for over 60% of outstanding global debt issued in these respective categories of issuer, and surprisingly, even European corporations have a dominant share in their category of issuer (private debt issued by non-financial corporations) in the international bond market, also above 50% (Figure 1.6a, first column).

It is impressive to notice how quickly EU market share has evolved in the mere six years since the introduction of the euro. In value terms, the share captured by EU issuers in the international bond market rose from below 45% in 1999 to over 55% by end-2004; the market share held by EU issuers of international debt securities rose about 15 percentage points, and by nearly the same number (although nearly tripling) in terms of global domestic debt securities outstanding (Figure 1.6b). True, domestic debt securities issued by EU entities have fallen since 1999, but this is primarily due to the mixture of fiscal consolidation in the EU and the rapidly developing government debt markets in underdeveloped countries.

Figure 1.6a EU market share in global international debt securities markets

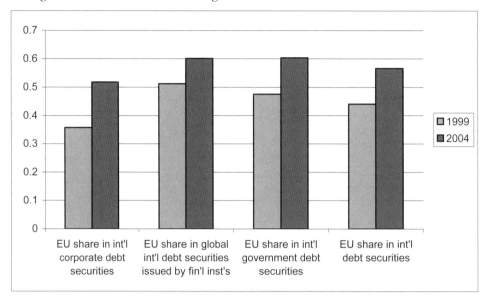

Figure 1.6b EU market share in global domestic debt securities markets

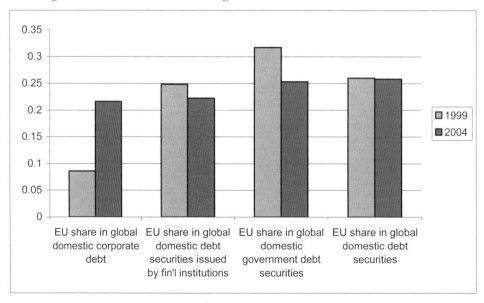

Source: Authors' own calculations using BIS data.

ii.   Net issuance of international debt securities

As can be seen from Figure 1.7, net issuance of international bonds by EU issuers displays an interesting pattern in comparison with issuers from other countries over the period 1993-2004. What is immediately evident is the reduced net issuance that resulted from the disciplinary measures imposed by the Maastricht criteria in the run-up to EMU from 1993 until 1999. In 1999, there is a sharp break in the trend, as net issuance of international bonds by EU issuers all of a sudden rose dramatically relative to the rest of the world.

Figure 1.7 Share of net issuance of international debt securities, by region

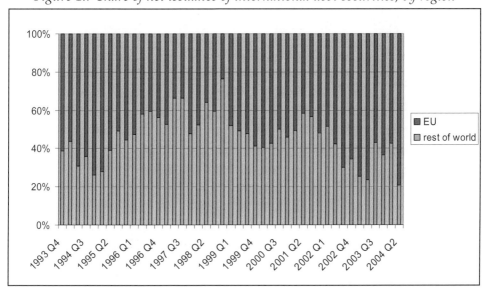

Source: Authors' own calculations from BIS data.

The recent dominance of EU issuers in total issuance of international debt securities can be attributed to two main causes: on the one hand, net issuance was unusually strong in the EU in 2002, 2003 and in the second half of 2004 by recent historical standards, reaching up to 80% of world quarterly net issuance; on the other hand, in the rest of the world, net issuance deviated significantly on the downside from the values one would expect if one would have extrapolated the historical trend line. In 2003, however, net issuance was lower in the EU compared to the two previous years, while in the rest of the world, it was on its way back up, which explains why the EU's share in total issuance receded in 2003.

iii. Size of international bonds issued by EU entities

An interesting feature in the international bond market since 1999 is the increasing average value of bond issues – straights and convertibles in particular, which, although already rising before that date, have grown much faster after monetary union (Figure 1.8). Straight bonds – the largest source of debt financing in the EU – reached an average size of nearly €500 million in 2004, up from around €120 million in 1988. This trend is reflected even more strongly in the average size of convertibles, which have grown from around €180 million to over €600 million in value over the same period. Finally, fixed rate issues are larger in size today than 15 years ago, but they have not displayed the same kind of steady rise in average value as straights and convertibles.

The increase in debt issue size is not surprising in light of the introduction of a common currency and is due to several factors: first, the cross-border consolidation that was expected to occur as a result of the single currency. As a result, mergers and acquisitions activity mushroomed, in effect creating a market for takeover, LBO and joint-venture financing. Also, issuers could now appeal to investors across the eurozone, facilitating access to debt financing and allowing for larger funding programmes that would previously have saturated local demand.

Figure 1.8 Average value of issue by bond type (€ millions)

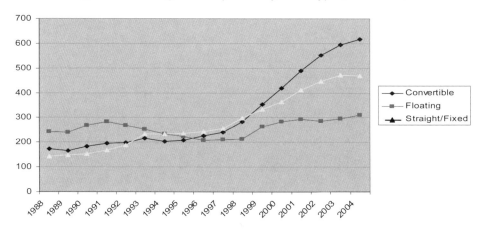

Source: Authors' own calculations with sample international bond market data provided by ISMA.

iv.   Evolutions in debt securities maturities

Maturities tend to increase as firms become more leveraged (Schiantarelli & Sembenellli, 1997). This result is intuitive, since firms with high short-term debt to total assets are likely to face refinancing problems, which may even result in severe liquidity shortages. Empirical tests have revealed an inverse relationship between maturity and firm indebtedness, at least up until a certain point. Beyond this point, the relationship becomes non-monotonic, as very highly-leveraged firms are more likely to default than firms with little debt, pushing anxious investors to demand the firm to issue short-term paper. Part of the push towards greater leveraging may be due to the greater institutional investor participation in capital markets fostered by the deregulation of the investment fund industry in the EU. Although acknowledging that research on the influence of institutional investors on firm leveraging is inconclusive, Davis (2002) cites a study by Firth (1995) that demonstrates empirically that the increasing presence of institutional investors encourages firms to leverage up.

Some of these theories may explain why the average maturities of debt securities issued by European entities, both official and private, in the international bond market have risen across the board between 1990 and 2003 (except for Sweden and Greece, where the maturities are weighted by issue size; see Figure 1.9). Some countries, especially Finland and the United Kingdom, have seen considerable lengthening of maturities of debt issued by entities registered in those countries, a rise of more than, and close to, four years, respectively. Other EU countries, such as Italy, the Netherlands and Belgium, have also witnessed non-negligible rises in the average maturity of international bonds issued by national entities. According to our ISMA sample, the average maturity across all issuer types and issue types rose from about 8.75 years in 1988 to around 10.75 years in 2004 (see Figure 1.10).

Another possible driver of the lengthening maturity structure of corporate debt in the EU is related to the widening and greater diversified investor base as a result of the single currency area. In the captive national markets, issuers had to respond to domestic investors' preferences when organising borrowing programmes. Until recently, it was by and large banks that held the lion's share of corporate debt. Because banks prefer to match closely their assets and liabilities, and because banks' liabilities are mostly short-term, they also prefer to hold assets with relatively short duration.

Figure 1.9 Eurobond maturities by issuer nationality

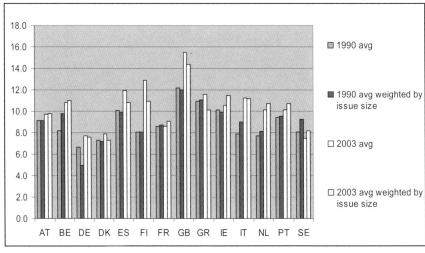

Source: Authors' own calculations with data on international debt issues provided by the International Securities Market Association (ISMA).

Figure 1.10 International bond maturities

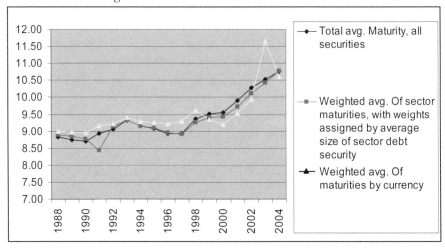

Source: Authors' own calculations with data on international debt issues provided by the International Securities Market Association (ISMA).

The close link between duration and maturity suggests that traditional banks with large deposit activities would prefer to hold debt with shorter maturities. But as former 'foreign' markets in the EU became part of the enlarged domestic market, life insurance and pension funds, which previously had been very constrained in their investment activities by limits to their exposure to foreign exchange risk, were free to hold assets across the EU. As a result, and compounded by the ongoing disintermediation, this trend has meant that more debt has ended up in the hands of investors that have long-term liabilities, and who will prefer to match them with long-term assets. With the demand for corporate bonds increasing as the 'home bias' phenomenon in portfolio management diminished greatly within the EU, it became cheaper for firms to issue long-term debt, so one would expect average maturities to rise subsequent to the introduction of a single currency. This seems to be the case, as seen in the figure above, although there are countervailing trends when one breaks down the average maturities by bond type.

In the international bond market, an interesting trend has been the impressive reduction in the maturity of convertible debt over the past 15 years (Figure 1.11). Whereas the average maturity of convertible issues was 14 years in 1988, it is below eight years today. Dutordoit & Van de Gucht (2004) estimate the average maturity for outstanding convertible debt issued by EU firms is 6.71 years and the median value is 5.48 years. This development may warrant further research, since the trend is pronounced, monotonic[10] and goes against the general trend of rising maturities observed in debt issued by EU entities in the international bond market.

Figure 1.11 Maturities of bond types

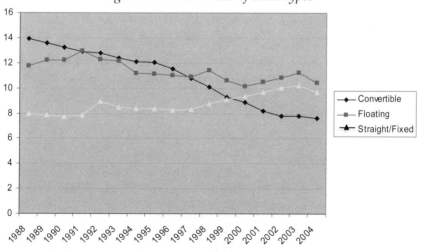

---

[10] A monotonic curve indicates the presence of a trend that is not broken by any lapses in the opposite direction, whether brief or prolonged or rare or common.

While some governments have been taking advantage of the lower financing costs ushered in by monetary union to lengthen the maturity structure of their debt (e.g. Spain, Italy, Greece, Portugal and recent fiscal 'sinner' Germany) others have been consolidating debt at the long end and bringing the fulcrum back towards shorter maturities, in order to preserve credit ratings from deterioration (Table 1.3).

Table 1.3 Term to maturity of government debt in the euro area (years)

End of 1995	End of 1998	End of 1998	End of 2002	End of 2003
Austria	5.8	5.5	6	6.3
Belgium	-	-	6.1	5.9
Finland	-	4.8	4.5	3.9
France	6.3	6.3	5.9	5.9
Germany	4.9	6	6	6.3
Greece	-	3.9	6.1	6.3
Ireland	-	-	4.5	5.8
Italy	4.5	5.2	5.6	6.1
Luxembourg	-	7	2.3	1.9
The Netherlands	6.9	6.5	6.1	6
Portugal	-	3.8	4.5	4.3
Spain	3.7	5.4	6	6.1
Euro area	-	-	5.8	6

Source: Annual reports of euro area debt managers and Wolswijk & de Haan (2005).

v.   A new asset class: The issuance of ultra-long bonds

In recent months, European capital markets have witnessed the introduction of a new debt class: the ultra-long maturity segment, comprised of sovereign and corporate bonds with 50-year maturities.[11]

---

[11] Ultra-long bonds are not a novelty in the American corporate debt market. The Walt Disney Corporation emitted a 100-year 'Sleeping Beauty' bond in 1993, although it is callable any time after 2023. This was the first debt security with century maturity since 1954. The Disney issue was followed by several others, including IBM, J.C. Penney and Financial Security Assurance Holdings. But North American economic history gives even more outlandish examples: Republic National Bank issued a 1000-year bond on October 1997 but it was not the first of its kind, as these millennial issues had been used by railroads in the late 19th century (Karpoff, 2004). Telecom Italia was the pioneer in the corporate bond market, launching a 50-year €500 million debendeture, stretching the yield curve in the corporate bond market farther out and further cementing the ongoing

Naturally, market integration contributed significantly to the development of this new asset class. Yet it was not alone in triggering the mushrooming of ultra-long maturity bonds. Time-specific market conditions also play a role, as issuers try to lock in the financing advantages offered by historically low long-term interest rates. As Figure 1.12 indicates, long-term interest rates have been falling in tandem with short-term rates over the past four years amid sanguine inflationary expectations, reducing the costs of debt financing.[12]

Figure 1.12 Short and long-term interest rates in the euro area (%)

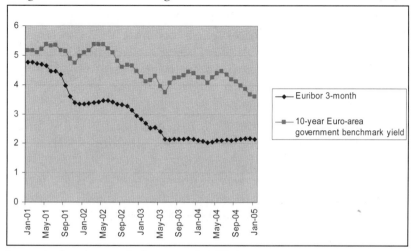

Source: Authors' own calculations with ECB data.

Yet it is especially enormous pressure from the demand side[13] combined with favourable supply conditions that has triggered the already high issuance of ultra-long bonds in both the government and corporate

---

transition from traditional bank-based financing to capital market access by European corporates.

[12] Low yields on long-term debt, particularly in an environment of rising short-term interest rates, have called market participants to evoke the possibility of a bubble in the bond markets (Greenspan's 'conundrum'), since markets do not seem to be properly pricing risk. Evidence for this can be gathered from the very narrow spread between benchmark government securities and riskier prospects.

[13] The 50-year French government issue, initially planned for a volume of €3-5 billion, was increased to €6 billion after demand exceeded €19 billion (Simensen, 2005b).

market segments, offering mutual benefits to both debt issuers and institutional investors: whereas EU governments are looking to take advantage of historically low interest rates to lock in cheap deficit financing over a horizon of half a century, government debt characterised by an ultra-long maturity structure will enable insurance firms and pension funds to generate a steady stream of income over extended periods.

There are signs that other European government issuers are quickly going to follow suit to exploit the favourable market conditions prevailing at the moment: Italy and the United Kingdom have announced plans to launch 50-year 'Methuselah' issues; even Greece recently floated a successful 30-year bond for the first time, at a surprisingly low 26 basis point spread over the German 30-year benchmark that will come to term around the same time.[14] Part of the reason governments such as the Greek and the Italian have been able to issue bonds with long and ultra-long maturities stems from the greater credibility of monetary policy in Europe.[15] Whereas the issuance of 50-year sovereign debt instruments would have been nearly unthinkable a generation ago, the more stable institutional framework, anchored by the constitutionally guaranteed independence of the ECB, has contributed in great part to its inception. These new maturities are also likely to impact the euro yield-curve, adding depth and creating new opportunities for trading along it. Additionally, adding another benchmark security at the tail of the curve enables investors to better price risk over long horizons.

Up until now, EU sovereign debt markets have been largely characterised by the domination of bonds with 10-year maturities, and overwhelmingly by bonds with maturities shorter than a quarter century, as seen in our sample dataset[16] from the international bond market: out of

---

[14] This low spread is all the more surprising, since the issue comes shortly after the finance ministry was rocked by revelations that Greece had been reporting falsified statistics on deficit levels for the better part of a decade. And yet demand for this issue was sufficient to push the government to the upper limit of the announced €3-5 billion range, at €5 billion (Simensen, 2005a).

[15] Institutional determinants of monetary policy credibility include full independence from political pressure, which is enshrined in the existing EU Treaties. Although the Federal Reserve is, strictly speaking, less independent than the European Central Bank, as measured by the Eijffinger-Schaling index for central bank independence. (See e.g. Eijffinger & Schaling, 1993).

[16] Courtesy of the International Securities Market Association (ISMA).

399 government debt securities from the international bond market, only 44, or just under 9%, have maturities longer than 25 years. A more comprehensive Merrill Lynch survey indicates that as of 2004, only 6% of eurozone sovereign bonds have maturities that exceed 25 years.[17] But there is little doubt that the trend of lengthening maturity structures in funding programmes will be extrapolated into the future, particularly in light of the challenges posed by the demographic deficit the European continent faces. The rapid ageing of the population means that the insurance industry, as well as pension funds, are looking to strengthen their balance sheets, given the enormous liabilities they face over the long term.

vi.   Recent trends in European sovereign debt markets

Vast amounts of research has been produced on European sovereign bond markets, especially analyses of yield convergence (see Baele et al., 2004). Accordingly, we limit ourselves to a brief overview and instead focus more attention on the corporate bond market.

Sovereign bond markets have long been, and continue to be, the most developed segment of European capital markets. For example, they still represent today a multiple of the outstanding value of corporate debt securities issued in the EU, figures that remain significantly higher in most EU countries than in the United States or the rest of the world (see Table 1.4).

For a long time, sovereign bonds represented the majority of total outstanding debt securities in Europe, although this is no longer the case today: debt securities issued by European financial institutions have now overtaken government debt as the single largest category of issuer in the EU bond market. This is the logical consequence of the pervasiveness of public deficits in Europe after the oil shocks and the need to fund these budgetary shortfalls efficiently at the lowest cost possible to the sovereign issuer. As a result, sovereign bond markets blossomed, their development not only spurred by the sheer size of public deficits, but also by direct government oversight of their operation and contributions to their design. Yet in the run-up to monetary union, fiscal deficits shrank as a logical consequence of the convergence programme, leading to smaller markets for government debt across the EU. More recently, as some member states, namely, Germany, France, Portugal and Italy, have plunged headlong into

---

[17] As reported in *The Economist* (2005).

protracted bouts of fiscal profligacy, public deficits are on the rise with a concomitant increase in government debt issuance. The trend described above is also due to the explosion in international debt issuance by European financial institutions.

*Table 1.4 Relative size of government and corporate debt markets**

Country	Austria	Belgium	Denmark	Finland	France	Germany	Greece	Ireland	Italy
Relative size	5.8	7.8	3.6	4.5	2.2	6.0	30.7	0.8	5.5

Netherlands	Portugal	Spain	Sweden	UK	Eurozone	EU-15	Japan	US	Rest of world
2.4	5.0	2.4	4.0	2.7	3.9	3.7	5.9	2.6	2.9

* Cell content represents the ratio of total value outstanding of government debt to corporate debt.

Source: Authors' own calculations with BIS data.

Because fiscal policy still falls within the remit of the EU member states, one cannot speak of a *European* sovereign debt market as such. Unlike the evolving European corporate debt market, government bond markets in Europe remain very much a national operation and continue to be tightly regulated by the national central banks and finance ministries for reasons having to do with monetary policy, financial stability and ensuring favourable conditions for the continued issuance of government debt. At over €1.3 trillion, Italy's government bond market remains the largest in the EU (and third largest in the world after the US and Japan), followed by Germany (€1 trillion), France (€900 billion) and the UK (€500 billion). Of all EU countries, Greece and Portugal have witnessed the most rapid growth in value of government debt outstanding, a total of over 110% in each case. Not surprisingly, they are accompanied by two other 'sinners' who have recently (and repeatedly) broken the Stability and Growth Pact, France and Germany, with respective growth rates of 64% and 91%.

Government bonds play an essential role in the proper functioning of the European repo market, since central government debt represents nearly 90% of collateral securing repo transactions (ISMA, 2004; Wolwijk & de Haan, 2005). In terms of the design of government funding programmes, their strategy still remains relatively simple in terms of the choice of debt instrument: the great majority of European sovereign bonds are bullet bonds with fixed coupons (Cheung et al., 2005).

Table 1.5 Government bonds

Country	Gov't debt securities outstanding, 1999-03 (€ billions)	Gov't debt securities outstanding, 2004-12 (€ billions)	Growth rate, 1999-2004
Austria	95.0	138.9	46%
Belgium	244.7	333.4	36%
Denmark	97.9	97.9	0%
Finland	69.5	97.9	41%
France	562.9	923.3	64%
Germany	555.8	1062.8	91%
Greece	106.0	224.4	112%
Ireland	28.0	34.4	23%
Italy	1050.6	1305.1	24%
Netherlands	169.8	226.6	33%
Portugal	46.4	97.2	110%
Spain	288.9	389.2	35%
Sweden	152.2	145.8	-4%
UK	408.4	522.3	28%
Eurozone	3217.5	4833.2	50%
EU-15	3875.9	5599.1	44%
US	3982.3	4261.0	7%
Japan	2520.5	5270.9	109%
World	11966.7	17773.8	49%
Rest of world	1587.9	2642.8	66%

Source: Authors' own calculations with BIS data.

vii. Recent trends in the European corporate bond market

It is especially private capital markets that have been the driving force behind the rapid evolution of European bond markets since the introduction of the euro, particularly in light of the fiscal consolidation that prevailed in the run-up to the single currency. In this section, we highlight developments in the EU corporate debt market and in the market for debt securities issued by financial institutions.

For a long time, the prevalence of relationship banking in financial intermediation in continental Europe meant that corporate debt markets remained significantly underdeveloped in contrast to the vibrant American market.[18] For example, at the time of the introduction of the euro, the

---

[18] As explained later in this chapter, there is one notable (and perhaps surprising) exception, France, which has a rather developed market for corporate debt relative to its continental neighbours.

European corporate debt market only accounted for 13% of the world market for private debt securities issued by non-financial corporations in contrast to a 56% US share. In other words, valued at €475 billion in 1999, the European corporate debt market was less than a quarter the size of its US counterpart (€2,020 billion).[19]

By the end of 2004, however, the global landscape of corporate debt markets had changed significantly. From 13% five years earlier, the EU market share had more than doubled, surging to 29%. In value terms, the amount outstanding of corporate debt securities issued by EU corporations reached €1,500 billion in 2004, or 74% of the US corporate debt market size (valued in euros), as opposed to less than 25% the value of the US market five years earlier.[20] Nevertheless, valued at $3,000 billion (€2,038 billion at current exchange rates), the corporate debt market in the United States still remains easily the largest in value terms, accounting for 40% of the total value of corporate debt securities in the world.[21] Today, within the EU, the leaders in the corporate bond market in value terms are France (€413.5 billion), Italy (€238.2 billion), the United Kingdom (€192.2 billion) and Germany (€175.7 billion).

The extraordinarily high growth rates recently registered by the European corporate bond market reflect the fact that it remains the fastest-growing segment of the European bond market, growing in value terms by 216% over the same time horizon and dwarfing the growth rate of the US market (30%).[22] Despite the high EU-15 average growth rate, some countries have seen nothing short of spectacular growth rates in the value of corporate bonds outstanding (Table 1.6). For example, the Italian corporate debt market has witnessed by far the most spectacular growth rate of all EU countries, growing by more than 1,300% since 1999. In addition, both the German and Irish markets grew by over 700%, and the Spanish one by over 300%.

---

[19] Authors' own calculations using BIS data.

[20] The US corporate debt markets was valued at $3,000 billion in December 2004. Violent movements in the €/$ exchange rates since 1999 mean that comparing the figures in terms of a single currency is risky, since exchange rate movements will affect the value of the US corporate debt market more than innate growth, artificially driving its value down (by up to 30%).

[21] As of December 2004 and measured in terms of euros, not US dollars.

[22] Authors' own calculations based on BIS data.

Table 1.6 Corporate bond market growth rate, 1999-2004

Austria	Belgium	Denmark	Finland	France	Germany	Greece	Ireland	Italy	Lux.
245%	228%	47%	137%	152%	715%	174%	704%	1360%	100%

Netherlands	Portugal	Spain	Sweden	UK	Eurozone	EU-15	Japan	US*
133%	97%	365%	74%	74%	283%	216%	35%	30%

* US figures were calculated in US dollars to prevent exchange rate movements from influencing the true rate of growth.

Source: Authors' own calculations; data from BIS and Eurostat.

In addition to being the largest corporate bond market in value terms, the US market also remained for a long time, the largest in relative terms, as a percentage of GDP, hovering around 25% in recent years. Yet over the last two years, due to phenomenal growth in its corporate debt market relative to GDP, Ireland has overtaken the US market in terms of relative size, reaching 29.5% of GDP, up from 6% of GDP in 1999 (!). The Irish corporate debt market doubled in value from the first quarter of 2003 to the fourth quarter of 2004 alone, growing from €21 billion to €43 billion. Aggregated across all EU countries, the value of corporate debt securities outstanding relative to GDP went from 6% of EU GDP in 1999 to 15.3% in 2004. Yet as seen in the Irish figures, the aggregate EU-15 statistic hides considerable variation in terms of the level of development, depth and liquidity of corporate bond markets. French firms have a longer tradition of tapping capital markets than their counterparts in other European countries, which may explain why, relative to GDP, France has traditionally been the leader in the European corporate debt market (ECB, 2004). In 2004, the amount outstanding of French corporate securities stood at 25% of GDP.

Table 1.7 Corporate bond market to GDP (as of December 2004)

Austria	Belgium	Denmark	Finland	France	Germany	Greece	Ireland	Italy	Lux.
10.2%	15.2%	14.1%	14.7%	25.1%	8.0%	4.4%	29.5%	17.6%	13.2%

Netherlands	Portugal	Spain	Sweden	UK	Eurozone	EU-15	Japan	US*
19.9%	14.3%	19.8%	12.9%	11.2%	16.5%	15.4%	19.2%	25.0%

* US figures were calculated in US dollars to prevent exchange rate movements from influencing the true rate of growth.

Source: Authors' own calculations; data from BIS and Eurostat.

As mentioned above, the speed of the transformation to arm's-length finance of some European countries with traditionally strong banking structures and correspondingly weak market infrastructures for arm's length finance, such as Italy and Germany, has been nothing short of phenomenal. In 1999, the value outstanding of corporate securities issued in Italy amounted to €16.3 billion, or 1.5% of GDP. By 2004, however, the Italian corporate bond market had grown to €238.2 billion, equivalent to 17.6% of Italian GDP. Likewise, the German corporate bond market, which only amounted to 1% of German GDP in 1999 (€21.6 billion), was equivalent to 8% of the same in 2004 (€175.8 billion). At only 4.4% of GDP, Greece retains the smallest corporate debt market in the EU-15 in both relative and absolute terms. Overall, relative to GDP, corporate bond markets have grown very quickly in the EU since 1999 (Figure 1.13). Coincidentally, it is perhaps surprising that the UK, which has a more market-oriented financial system than France, registers a lower ratio, only achieving 11.2% of GDP (although one must beware of exchange rate movements influencing this figure).

These developments illustrate an increased investor appetite for exposure to the credit of corporate entities, and in sharp contrast with the government bond segment, which is essentially part of the interest rate arena; this has been part of the dynamic increase in credit markets in general. Some of this increase can be attributed to the development of more sophisticated hedging techniques such as credit default swaps and comparatively low and stable inflation throughout the EU. At the extreme end of the credit spectrum is high-yield debt (also called junk bonds), which is sub-investment grade (below BBB), and it is characterised by higher returns and higher risk than in the investment grade corporate bond market. Default probabilities are elevated compared with investment-grade bonds, meaning a heightened risk of principal loss or missed coupon payments, risks for which investors require compensation at a premium over 'risk-free', and the essentially interest rate sensitive government securities. Though a fairly new concept itself (having only taken off in the United States in the 1980s), the market for high-yield corporate issues is a new segment in the European fixed income landscape, only arriving in Europe in the mid-1990s (De Bondt & Marqués-Ibáñez, 2005).

Figure 1.13 Corporate bond market relative to GDP, 1999-2004

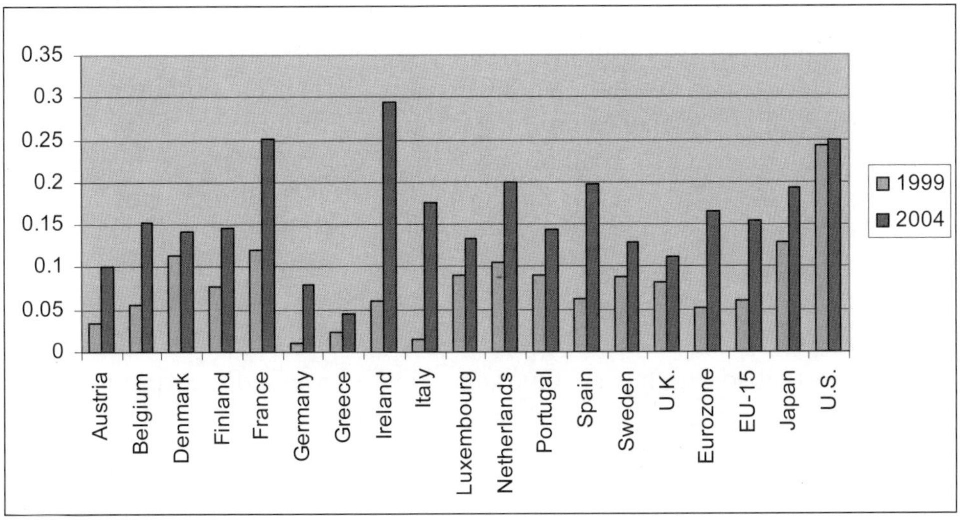

Source: Authors' own calculations; BIS and Eurostat data.

At times when equity returns are flat and bond yields are depressed in an environment of rising interest rates, the demand for high-yield debt rises, as has been the case in both the US and EU fixed income markets in recent months. Despite the rising demand for junk bonds – which has pinched yield spreads over government benchmarks to very low levels in comparison with historical trends (Figure 1.14) it is unlikely that the Drexel Burnham Lambert heydays of the 1980s will be revisited, especially in Europe, where the market is still nascent. Even in the US, which has the most developed market in the world for junk bonds, these latter only represent about 6% of the total US corporate bond market (De Bondt & Marqués-Ibáñez, 2005). As of late 2001, the value outstanding of high-yield corporate bonds issued in the EU was on trend to reach €25 billion by 2002 and their market share fluctuated between 3-4% of the total value of the European corporate bond market (De Bondt & Marqués-Ibáñez, 2005).

There are two types of junk bonds: those that are issued as junk and those existing issues that are downgraded to junk due to adverse credit events. The latter are known as 'fallen angels'. Most high yield bonds, including those issued by EU corporates, fall into the former category, that is, they are issued as securities rated below investment grade. In terms of ratings, B rated bonds seem to be in the majority at the time of issue, accounting for some 70% of new high-yield issues (see De Bondt & Marqués-Ibáñez, 2005).

Figure 1.14 High-yield bond spreads

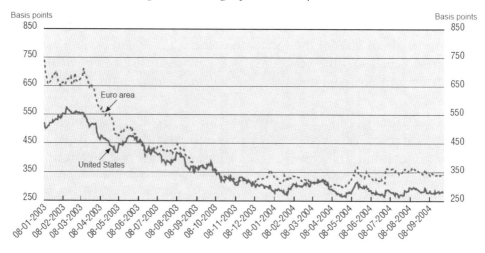

Source: OECD Financial Market Trends, October 2004.

To summarise, the European fixed income landscape has been radically transformed by phenomenal rates of growth in corporate bond markets since the introduction of the euro. The latter can be seen as the proximate cause of this fast-paced development, because since 1999, European corporate debt markets have been growing at several times that of those in the US and Japan, or even than those in the rest of the world, where the corporate bond segment in emerging markets have been growing rapidly.

viii. Covered bonds and securitised debt

Issuance of securitised debt has been rising quickly in Europe.[23] In 2001, a total of €153.6 billion worth of asset-backed securities were outstanding, growing to €243.6 billion by 2004, or an increase of 58% in three years.[24] The European securitisation market is dominated by the United Kingdom, and

[23] Europe here is defined as the EU-15 plus the following countries: Czech Republic, Poland, Switzerland and 'multinational', according to the European Securitisation Forum definition.

[24] Data on securitised debt in this section are kindly provided by Marco Angheben from the European Securitisation Forum.

housing prices are a vital pillar underpinning new issues. Mortgage-backed securities are the largest asset component in the European market, followed by asset-backed securities. Overall, outstanding securitised debt issues account for about 20% of the total value of the European bond market. By comparison, in 2003, the combined value of securitised debt in the then accession countries (now new member states) was only a tiny €3 billion (see Solans, 2004).

Pfandbriefe[25] account for nearly 30% of the German fixed income market and 68% of the European covered bond market (followed by Denmark, 15% and France, 6%).[26] Their attractiveness is derived from their very high degree of safety – not once in the past 100 years has an investor not fully recovered the value of his principal – the premium they yield over German government bonds, as well as their great liquidity.

New issues of securitised debt remain larger in the UK than in any other EU country, reaching a value of €76 billion in 2003 and accounting for 35% of the total value of the combined European asset-backed securities (ABS) and mortgage-backed securities (MBS) markets. Spain came in second with €37.84 billion, followed by Italy (€33.93 billion) and the Netherlands (€20.98 billion). The strong position of the UK is due primarily to the importance of its housing market for the overall performance of European securitised debt markets, reflected in the fact that 44% (€55.3 billion) of the European MBS market is backed by UK collateral. In terms of the origin of MBS collateral, the Netherlands and Spain are a distant second and third place, with respective market shares of only 14% and 13%.

Issuance in *Pfandbrief* markets grew quickly (13% year-on-year) in 2003, reaching a total of €236.2 billion. Not surprisingly, the German market accounted for the lion's share of new issues, but there is an underlying trend of internationalisation of the *Pfandbrief* as a popular debt instrument, since 81% of *Pfandbrief* issues originated in Germany in 2003, less than in previous years; likewise, in the *Jumbo Pfandbrief* segment, the internationalisation of the market has been even more rapid: by 2003, only 42% of all new issues originated in Germany, down from 50% the year before (VDH, 2004). A number of reforms to national legislation in several EU member states have helped to propel the increasing importance of the

---

[25] *Pfandbriefe* is a term for bonds that are secured by public sector or mortgage loans.

[26] Statistics from the New York Society of Securities Analysts.

covered bond market in Europe, in addition to the recent introduction of covered bond legislation in a few countries, such as Luxembourg, Finland and Italy (see Table 1.8).

The European securitisation market is characterised by the following specificities: it remains highly fragmented in Europe, in the sense that most deals are not multinational; large cross-country differences persist due to country-specific legal, tax and accounting frameworks and varying incentives for banks to package structured products (ECB, 2004).

Table 1.8 Recent legislative measures in EU member states addressing covered bonds

Year	Country	Action taken
1997	Luxembourg	Introduction of covered bond legislation, the *lettres de gage*. It was later reformed in 2000
1998	Germany	Reform of the Mortgage Banking Act (HBG)
1999	Finland	Introduction of covered bond legislation
	France	Revision of the law on obligations foncières
2001	Spain	First repackaged covered bond, *cédulas hipotécarias*, which are backed by mortgages
2002	Ireland	Law on covered bonds came into force – asset covered securities
	Germany	Reform of Mortgage Banking Act and the Public Sector Pfandbrief Act (OePG)
2003	Spain	First issuance of covered bonds backed by public sector assets – *cédulas territoriales*
	UK	First structured covered bond issued by HBOS
	Austria	First issuance of jumbo covered bonds called *fundierte Anleihen* by Kommunalkredit
2004	Germany	Another reform of the Mortgage Banking Act and Public Sector *Pfandbrief* Act
	Sweden	Revised covered bond legislation in force since 1 July
2004+	Portugal	Reform of covered bond legislation
	Italy	Introduction of covered bond legislation
	Austria	Reform of the three *Pfandbrief* laws
	Germany	Creation of one *Pfandbrief* framework which will replace the three existing laws

Source: UBS; taken from *Euromoney* magazine, November 2004.

2. Bond and Bond Derivatives Market Structure

2.1 Primary markets

i. Bond listings

Mostly for historical reasons linked to the development of the international bond market, the vast majority of bonds listed in the EU have chosen Luxembourg or London as their regulatory regime[27] (although London is the undisputed 'home' of the international bond market if secondary market activity is considered). Both are characterised by extensive disclosure requirements for first-time listings, annual reports and other transparency obligations.[28] As of May 2005, Luxembourg was still by far the location of choice for bond listings (primarily Eurobonds, which

---

[27] For more information on EU regulation concerning the primary market and especially the prospectus directive, see chapter 3.

[28] See Esho et al. (2004) To get an idea of the costs of listing an issue on the international bond market, the following data from the Luxembourg stock exchange are useful. The fee structure is composed of three parts: a visa, listing and maintenance fee. First-time listings cost €1,500 for first-time ordinary issuers, €1,375 for supranational issuers but only €625 and €560 for subsequent listings. These fees apply equally for straights and convertibles multi-tranche issues and debt securities programmes. Bonds with warrants are considerably more expensive: €2,125 and €1,935 for ordinary and supranational issuers, respectively, for first listings and €1,250 and €1,120, respectively, for subsequent listings. Listing fees for all types of fixed income securities and all issuers are identical at €600, except for debt securities programmes (€1,200 for first listing). Maintenance fees vary more across fixed income securities types but tend to increase with the size of the issue. By way of comparison, the listing costs for equities are significantly greater, with a fee of €2,500 for first listings and €1,250 for subsequent listings, and maintenance fees that are multiples of those for fixed income securities.

comprised all but four of the total bonds listed), with a total of 25,573 compared with the next three largest, the London Stock Exchange, Deutsche Börse and the Irish Stock Exchange, with 10,454, 8,861 and 7,490 listings, respectively.[29] By contrast, the new member states only account for a miniscule fraction of bond listings in the EU. The average number of bonds listed on Eastern European exchanges is 84.[30] International bonds generally are not listed in the new member states, as the total for the region's exchanges is a mere 18 issues. Overall, there are 69,323 total bond listings in the EU today.[31] Only a small proportion of these bonds, however, trade on exchange.

ii.   Underwriting

In the aggregate, European investment banks hold strong positions as bookrunners in the European bond primary market, particularly in euro-denominated supranational bonds, agency bonds, covered bonds and corporate bonds, as the following brief summary of the 2004 league tables for primary market activity indicates.[32] The top four bookrunners for corporate bonds issued in euros were all European banks.[33] Together, they accounted for a market share of 32.3% in euro corporate bonds in 2004.[34] It is worth noting that 85% of the EU non-government bonds are underwritten and traded in London (TBMA, 2005b) In the jumbo covered bonds (*Pfandbriefe*) market, all the top five, and seven out of the top 10 bookrunners were European banks, accounting for a combined market share of 57.7%. Likewise for the category of all covered bonds, where seven of the top 10 were European banks, with a combined market share of 52.3%. Six out of the top 10 bookrunners in both agencies and

---

[29] Federation of European Securities Exchanges (FESE) statistics (www.fese.be).

[30] Based on the average number of bonds listed on the Bratislava, Budapest, Ljubljana, Prague and Warsaw exchanges only, so the figure may not be exact, particularly as the Baltic exchanges (Tallinn, Riga and Vilnius) have all been acquired by the Scandinavian OMX Group.

[31] www.fese.be.

[32] The following data are drawn from the league tables published in the 8 January 2005 edition of *IFR Magazine*.

[33] Deutsche Bank, BNP Paribas, Barclays and Société Générale, in that order.

[34] In addition to these banks, ABN Amro, Dresdner Kleinwort Wasserstein and HSBC also figured in the top 10 for this category, bringing the total to 45.7% for all these banks alone.

supranationals were European, with respective shares of 35.6% and 59.4%. European banks' performance was weaker in the primary market for sovereign debt issues: only one out of the top five bookrunners in euro-denominated sovereign debt was a European bank. (Deutsche Bank, ranked first with a 9.7% share) and there were only five European banks in the top 10, accounting for only 27% of the market.

Underwriting in the international bond market remains fiercely competitive, as reflected in the regular churning of lead managers. In their interesting work on the determinants of underwriter spreads in the Eurobond market, Esho, Kollo and Sharpe (2004) offer important insights. For example, private placements command significantly smaller spreads than public offerings.[35] Private placements are attractive to issuers: household name firms with strong credit (and issuing) reputations that dominate the international bond market can better tap the markets at the time of their choice (e.g. to take advantage of a temporary window of low interest rates) with a (quick) private placement instead of alternative distribution channels. Spreads are lower for: bearer bonds, whose anonymity provisions are attractive to potential buyers; underwriting services from non-bulge bracket firms, since the name recognition of the most established players comes at a premium and offers the issue credibility due to the attached monitoring, signalling and certification services (Esho et al., 2004; Chemmanur et al., 1994); bonds issued in US dollars; longer maturity issues; and Eurobonds governed by English, as opposed to New York, law (Esho et al., 1999).[36] Since the advent of EMU, underwriting fees have fallen considerably in Europe. Prior to the introduction of the euro, Eurobond issues denominated in European legacy currencies commanded fees of nearly 0.2% higher than those denominated in US dollars; however, since 1999, the situation has reversed: Eurobonds denominated in euros command smaller underwriting fees (Melnik & Nissim, 2004).

---

[35] In the Eurobond market, outright fees are usually not charged to issuers by the underwriters. Rather, they are subsumed into the spread. Intermediation costs are recuperated by the underwriter purchasing the entire issue (in the case of a bought deal) from the issuer at a price below the offering rate, and selling to investors at a profit.

[36] The logic here is that the English system is superior according to the cited study for the renegotiation of contract terms with the borrower in the face of default.

Finally, one must note that even though their main activity is in the primary market, lead managers also play an important role in secondary markets by helping interested parties identify holders of bonds issued in bearer form, thus contributing substantially to enhancing the overall liquidity of the market.

iii.   Public-private cooperation in the primary market – The development of primary dealers

Concerning the primary market for government debt securities, EU governments have increasingly turned to private intermediaries to help them place their debt issues, such that all EU countries except for Germany now distribute public debt issues through primary dealers (ECB, 2005a). In addition the issuers often require their primary dealers to offer firm quotes in the secondary market as a condition of their primary dealership. Primary dealers are reluctant to risk their privileged status, as they typically receive several benefits from the issuer; which may vary from having the right to buy additional new issues of bonds the day following an auction at preferential prices, to arranging securitisations or providing the relevant government with advisory services. This public-private collaboration is typically formed around supposedly mutually beneficial gentlemen's agreements or contracts between sovereign issuers and market-makers, which detail the mutual obligations of each party. A good example of how certain member state's treasuries watch closely over such agreements is the so-called MTS 'Liquidity Pact', which is discussed in the next section. In order to better manage the risks associated with launching innovative issues that have not yet stood the test of investor demand, European governments have turned increasingly to syndication, as in the case of Italian index-linked and 50-year bonds (ECB, 2004).

iv.   Technology in the primary market

Primary debt markets in Europe have not remained unaffected by technological developments. Almost all EU countries have adopted electronic auction or tap issuance systems so that the government debt issuance process has become very nearly fully automated (ECB, 2004).[37] Electronic trading has spread to the grey market as well. Today,

---

[37] The ECB study cites the UK, Slovakia and the Czech Republic as examples of EU countries that have yet to move to automate primary market activity in their sovereign issues.

Telematico, the same fixed income Escreen-based system that is used to power the MTS system, allows the trading of securities for announced government debt issues eligible for trading on the MTS system, but whose auctions have not yet been held. Access to these parts of the relevant MTS system is restricted to the primary dealers of that issuer. The introduction of electronic trading brings greater transparency, efficiency and liquidity to the grey market, which fulfils several useful functions. These include: providing important information to the issuer about the true value of the security it is about to offer in the market; protecting members of the primary dealer group from participating in badly priced deals and suffering losses when placing the issue; and allowing investors and regulators to better monitor prices and to detect cases of price discrimination in placements (Levich, 1998). The Telematico market only allows trading until the auction date, whereupon the issue will graduate to the regular MTS trading screens.

v. *Syndicated credits*

For the sake of comparison with primary market activities for debt issues, we briefly describe trends in the syndicated credit market. The US continues to dominate the global market for syndicated credits. In 2004, the total number and volume of syndicated loans were 7,214 and $2.658 trillion or €2.2 trillion at current exchange rates.[38] Of these, the US market accounted for 3,481 loans for $1.332 trillion, or more than half the global market in value terms. By contrast, combined EU loans (including the new member states) totalled $796.8 billion, led by the UK, which accounted for 29.8% of the EU total.[39] The total number of syndicated loans in the EU in 2004 was 1107, or less than one-third the US total. In other words, the average size of EU syndicated credits ($724.4 million) was significantly larger – nearly twice the size of the average US loan ($382.6 million).[40] EU banks maintained a strong standing as bookrunners in the syndicated credits market with 7 out of the top 10 performers, accounting for a share of 47.7% among the share of 98.9% controlled by the top 10 bookrunners for syndicated credits.

---

[38] Data are drawn from the league tables published in the 8 January 2005 edition of *IFR Magazine*.

[39] Authors' calculations based on the league tables mentioned in footnote above.

[40] Authors' calculations based on the league tables mentioned in footnote above.

2.2   Secondary markets

i.   *The emergence and consequences of the MTS trading system*

The development of secondary markets for government bonds in Europe was spurred not only by the sheer size of the accumulated public deficits of the past three decades, but also by government efforts to better manage this large stock of debt. Enhancing the liquidity of the inter-bank segment of secondary markets was seen to be an important step in rendering government securities more attractive to investors, and ensuring the uptake of new issues by the primary dealers essential to reduce the costs of funding debt for the sovereign borrower. Owing to its perennial and large deficits, Italy became the third-largest sovereign debt market in the world (after the United States and Japan), and the Italian market is today worth some € 1.3 trillion. Due to the requirement to employ primary dealers, and most significantly monitor their market-making performance, Italy was the first European country to utilise electronic trading in its government bonds with the creation of an inter-dealer platform called MTS S.p.a. (Mercato dei Titoli de Stato) in 1988. The experiment was generally seen to be a success, since the system managed to attract a great majority of most secondary market activity for Italian *Buoni del Tesoro* away from the exchange and from other over-the-counter venues and was recognised as having improved the liquidity of Italian government bonds (see ECB, 2005b).

Estimates differ as to exactly what percentage of trading volume was captured by MTS SpA: an IBRD/IMF (2001) handbook on government debt markets suggests a figure as high as 90% while an ECB study (Cheung et al., 2005) suggests it is closer to 65%.[41] Nevertheless, some commentators will argue that by making it a requirement for the primary dealers to quote two-way prices on the MTS system, it effectively created a *mandatory* pool of liquidity, removing the incentive of the primary dealers to risk capital by trading Italian government bonds elsewhere. In any case, finance ministries in other EU member states watched in interest and envy as the Italian system lowered borrowing costs and seemed to improve liquidity in the secondary market, while giving the Italian government the opportunity to closely watch the activities of primary dealers. Yet it is important to note that liquidity in the secondary market for Italian treasuries was not enhanced solely by the introduction of MTS. A good example is the July

---

[41] But the ECB study takes its figure from an older Italian Treasury document published in 2000.

1997 decision to do away with revealing traders' identities provided with quotes and to move to anonymity, which had a beneficial impact on liquidity in the Italian market.[42]

The MTS eventually was extended to EU-15 member states' bond trading except for the UK (which at the time placed no requirement to quote specific spreads on its primary dealers), Sweden and Luxembourg.[43] Many of these platforms quickly came to dominate trading in the inter-dealer market for government debt securities in their respective countries, achieving high market shares.[44] Besides replication of the Italian system in all but three member states, the London-based EuroMTS was launched in 1999 as a pan-European platform for trading in benchmark securities issued from 11 sovereign issuers[45] and 4 quasi-government issuers.[46] This and related EuroMTS markets also employ mandatory quoting and are owned by MTS SpA.

The following paragraphs summarise market-making requirements that are standardised across the system and enshrined in the Liquidity Pact, an informal agreement between primary dealers and government issuers that is monitored by the latter (see MTS, 2003). Liquidity providers must display two-way quotes for two-way proposals within a defined maximum spread and for a minimum size for at least five hours per day for all the bonds it was assigned. A market-maker is free to make and take prices in

---

[42] See Scalia & Vaca (1997).

[43] After Italy introduced the system in 1988, the MTS system was extended to Austria (2003), Belgium (2000), Denmark (2003), Finland (2002), France (2000), Germany (2001), Greece (2003), Ireland (2002), the Netherlands (1999), Poland (2004), Portugal (2000) and Spain (2002).

[44] The notable exceptions were the Spanish bond market, which is dominated by local brokers and the state-sponsored Senaf system, and the Greek government-owned HDAT system for Greek bonds.

[45] Namely, Austria, Belgium, Finland, France, Germany, Greece, Ireland, Italy, The Netherlands, Portugal and Spain. In addition, Polish government bonds are traded on the system. In addition, a new system, New Euro MTS, was designed specifically to trade government debt securities of the 10 new EU member states.

[46] Namely, Depfa, the European Investment Bank (EIB), Freddie Mac and Kreditanstalt für Wiederaufbau (KfW) (see www.euromts-ltd.com). But a separate platform also exists for trading quasi-government debt, MTS Quasi-government. Requirements to trade on this platform are: 8 supporting market-makers, at least a AA rating, and a minimum issue size of €2 billion.

any bond on the system at its discretion, provided it satisfies its obligations in respect of the bonds it has been allocated. Spreads and proposal size obligations can vary between maturity buckets and between benchmark and liquid issues. To get an idea of the nature of market-making obligations on MTS platforms and the constraints they impose, Table 2.1 highlights the specifications of the range of bid-ask spreads to which primary dealers must adhere in the market for Italian Treasuries, or *Buoni del Tresoro Poliennali* (BTPs).

Table 2.1 Spreads on different maturity tranches on MTS

Segment	Bucket	Liquid (ticks)	Not Liquid (ticks)
BTP	A (<3.5yrs)	4	7
	B (3.5 - 6.5yrs)	5	12
	C (6.5 - 13.5yrs)	7	16
	D (>13.5yrs)	20	45

Source: MTS group.

The number of market-makers for government debt securities varies across EU member states. Germany (38 participants in the primary market)[47] has the most of any country, despite (or perhaps because of) not having very demanding primary dealer requirements, and Ireland the least (10). Italy, which has a larger outstanding debt than Germany, has 31 participating market-makers on the MTS Italy system. Due to the diversity of issuers and large number of primary dealers in Europe, it is perhaps not surprising that overall the EuroMTS platform has 51 market-makers. Only Deutsche Bank is active as a market-maker on all 15 MTS platforms (including the non-sovereign EurocreditMTS). Deutsche Bank also happens to be a large player in EU primary markets, capturing the largest market share in 2004 for bookrunning in both Euromarket issues and bonds denominated in euros (respective shares are 7.5% and 7.8%; totals are €127 billion and €80 billion; and number of issues are 503 and 303).[48] Citigroup is present on all systems except for MTS Denmark. A number of large players are present as market-makers on many MTS platforms.

---

[47] Members of the Bund Issues Auction Group as of 11 August 2005, published by the Deutsche Bundesbank.

[48] IFR Magazine, 8 January 2005: league tables from Thomson Financial.

A recent study by the ECB (Cheung et al., 2005) comes to interesting conclusions about the microstructure of trading on the MTS trading system(s): quoted bid-ask spreads do not differ much at all between EuroMTS and the national platforms; MTS markets are very deep, that is, the transaction costs for large orders, measured as the bid-ask spread, hardly differ from small orders.[49] The former result would appear to suggest that liquidity does not vary much between the national trading platforms and the centralised EuroMTS platform, a sign that the government debt markets in Europe have become significantly more integrated in recent years, and especially since the introduction of MTS. Alternatively, it is also possible that this is a product of the mandatory quoting obligations placed on the dealers, since market-making obligations are standardised across the system.

As a result, some observers have argued that the perceived depth of the MTS system is only an illusion, since it may be because liquidity is artificially standardised across these platforms by the similar or identical market-making requirements enshrined in the Liquidity Pact. A consequence of this argument is that Citigroup's controversial trade-exploiting liquidity imbalances – made public in August 2004 – between the cash and futures markets was not such a terrible thing to happen after all. In fact, they might even have improved market efficiency if they had been carried out as intended – albeit this contention remains highly controversial.[50] The unique market model created and perpetuated by the mandatory quoting system meant that dealers on multiple MTS platforms were exposed to having their prices accepted in a wide variety of bonds simultaneously. It still remains difficult to tell whether liquidity on the MTS system is design-induced or generic. If indeed liquidity in the system

---

[49] For their sample time period, the authors of the ECB study find that in Italian 10-year benchmarks, quoted spreads for a €5 million trade averaged about 3 basis points, whereas a trade of €25 million only paid a slightly more (less than 4 basis points), despite the size of the order (Cheung et al., 2005, p. 16).

[50] As argued in an opinion piece in *The Banker*, 2 September 2004: "In 2004, markets cannot operate on the basis of a gentleman's agreement." Evidently, regulators could not contain their anger, but they were powerless to act since the market abuse Directive had not yet been implemented. And whether the trade actually constituted true market abuse is debatable. Nevertheless, despite criminal charges being dropped, the Financial Services Authority has indicated it will impose a fine of between $10-$15 million to indicate its disapproval of the "lack of internal controls" (Bradberry, 2005).

were but an illusion, it would quickly evaporate for larger orders, which has not proven to be the case. Nevertheless, overall volumes on the various MTS platforms have decreased since August 2004. Some of this decline may be attributed to imperfections in the system revealed by the Citigroup trade, but prevailing market conditions in an unstable macroeconomic environment has also led to a fall in volumes across most electronic platforms and a concomitant rise in the use of voice broking (Bearing Point, 2005).

ii.   Electronisation of trading

The introduction of the MTS system was but a piece (albeit a large one) in the broader context of a rapid ongoing transformation of secondary markets due to the rise of electronisation of trades in the inter-bank as well as bank-to-institutional investor (sovereign) bond market segments. Even in the corporate debt market, the effects of electronisation are gradually beginning to be felt, although predominantly limited to large, investment grade issues. According to The Bond Market Association, there are over 23 multi-dealer platforms for electronic trading of corporate and sovereign debt instruments in Europe today. Of these, 11 are national MTS trading platforms for sovereign debt, 3 are non-MTS sovereign debt platforms and 8 are hybrids trading both types of instruments (TBMA, 2005a). Notable in the inter-bank (B2B) wholesale bond trading space is ICAP/BrokerTec, which trades approximately $450 billion per day.[51]

In the bank-to-institutional investor (B2C) space, a different market model dominates. TradeWeb, owned by Thomson Financial, has the largest market share of electronically-traded government debt. The Tradeweb system is based on the Request for Quote (RFQ) model – not the market-maker model of MTS. In this model dealers are not required to make firm prices continuously, but only in response to requests from investors (who

---

[51] The majority of this volume is in euro 'repo' (repurchase agreements, whereby buyer and seller agree to repurchase the bonds at a future date, usually at a slightly higher price, economically representing a rate of interest), euro 'basis' trades (where a bond is traded against an opposite and corresponding position in a futures contract of similar maturity) and US Treasury bonds traded in Europe. This very high electronic daily turnover, combined with that of other platforms, such as eSpeed, dwarfs the notional volume of trades on the MTS systems, but primarily in relation to bonds or transaction types that are not the subject of primary dealer agreements.

can make the same request to multiple dealers simultaneously). It is an interesting question, and so far unexplained, why this model has proved far more successful in meeting the needs of institutional investors than the continuous quote model which dominates the B2B space. However, the answer may prove crucial to the further development of electronic trading.

Electronic trading is usually successful in capturing market shares where standardised products are the norm (Andersen & Baertelsen, 2004). However, electronic trading is also sensitive to extremes of price volatility, and there is still a significant amount of business traded via voice brokers or directly between counterparties. The introduction of the euro was a powerful catalyst in standardising government debt instruments. To begin with, the great majority of EU government debt is issued in a common currency, meaning that debt managers in EU finance ministries have for the first time entered into direct competition with each other. Due in part to the introduction of a common trading system, benchmark issues at least have become more aligned in the EU, with similar issue sizes, maturities and coupon rates, increasing the comparability (and thus competition) between various sovereign debt issues.

Generally, the introduction of electronic trading screens has substantially improved liquidity on secondary markets for sovereign debt in the EU: trading volumes have risen significantly in recent years and bid-offer spreads have fallen (Andersen & Baertelsen, 2004). These trends have been accompanied by a reduction in the variability of trading volume as a result of the MTS system.

Historically, one of the key distinctions differentiating the market structure of fixed income from equities is that a vast majority of fixed income transactions took place over-the-counter, or outside the exchange. This division is perhaps blurring due to the comparative focusing of the largest bond markets in a reduced number of venues. Although the vast majority of bond trading in Europe is still conducted off-exchange, the fixed income landscape has evolved with technological progress, in the sense that bond trading has become more centralised, while still remaining a hybrid model: the introduction of electronic trading and the capacity of these platforms to allow for multiple parties to post and view quotes has reduced – although certainly not eliminated – bilateral negotiations (especially not in heterogeneous or illiquid securities). Thus, the nature of the bond asset class itself makes the complete transfer to an exchange environment unlikely, and the hybrid model is very likely to stay.

After the explosion of electronic trading systems that occurred in the late 1990s and early years of the present decade, there is now more or less a consensus that a period of rationalisation will follow. As of 2004, there were 74 electronic fixed income trading platforms in the EU and US combined (31 are based in Europe), a six-fold increase since 1997, when there were only 11 (TBMA, 2004). At the same time, exchanges are positioning themselves to expand aggressively in the OTC market, as evidenced by the recent acquisition of a majority share of MTS SpA by Euronext and Borsa Italiana and the development of Eurex Bonds and Eurex Repo. This may lead to a possible future showdown with dealers as they encroach on the latter's traditional strongholds. In the context of the MiFID review, Goldfinger (2003) suggests a repeat of the clashes that resulted from dealers and exchanges sparring for control over the policy-influenced future of market organisation in the early 1990s during negotiations over the initial investment services directive (ISD).

iii.   Trading activity in the European sovereign and corporate debt markets[52]

Altogether, the MTS system comprises the single largest market for the trading of outright cash eurozone public debt, achieving €18.4 trillion traded on all MTS platforms in the cash and repo markets in 2004.[53] As of 2004, €25 billion in government bonds traded every day on the MTS system alone. This sum is believed to have represented 60% of electronic inter-dealer trading in European sovereign debt at that time.[54] If this estimate is accurate, on average roughly €40 billion in EU government bonds were traded daily in the inter-dealer electronic market alone. It is estimated that this represented 65% or so of the whole inter-dealer segment of the market, making the total daily turnover somewhere in the region of €62 billion. In

---

[52] We recognise that the data in this section are outdated, as most of them are from 2004, but for the sake of consistency in, and comparability of, the data, we could not bring them fully up to date. As market dynamics evolve at a brisk pace, the figures in this section may not deliver an accurate picture of what is actually prevailing in the markets today. For example, there is evidence that volumes on electronic trading platforms have fallen quite substantially over the past 18 months.

[53] See www.mtsgroup.org.

[54] This estimate was obtained through telephone conversations with European sovereign debt market participants.

other words, although electronic trading represented the lion's share of government bond trading in the EU in 2004, a far from negligible portion of the outright cash bond market was still intermediated by voice brokers. There is even evidence that voice broking has been making a comeback in the European fixed income world in 2005, as volatile market conditions have lessened the attractiveness of electronic platforms.[55]

Despite the relative sizes of the amount of debt issued by eurozone governments and the US Treasury,[56] the activity in the secondary market is considerably less in European debt; it is estimated that the inter-dealer market in US Treasury instruments is approximately $200 billion per day. This may be due to the fractured nature of eurozone debt issuance in comparison with the more liquid bond future and interest rate swaps markets. In the eurozone the interest rate benchmark curve can reasonably be regarded as the swap curve, while in relation to the USD, it is the US Treasury bond curve that dictates the cost of borrowing.

Electronic dealer-client volume in Europe is smaller than in the inter-dealer market, but it is increasing; it is now estimated at €22 billion daily by a recent study.[57] Total electronic trading in government securities in the EU can therefore be estimated to be somewhere around €62 billion a day. As electronic trading is generally believed to represent about 75% of trading in government debt in Europe (80% according to The Bond Market Association and 70% according to Celent Communications), the aggregate total daily turnover in the European secondary market for government debt securities can be estimated at €83 billion for 2004. A 2004 study by Celent yields a similar estimate: €84 billion. An €85 billion daily market translates into a yearly turnover of some €21.2 trillion.[58]

As one can see from Figure 2.1, voice brokering is more important, both in value and percentage terms, in the inter-dealer market than in dealer-client transactions (35% and 31%, respectively), although in

[55] This observation derives from conversations with various market participants.

[56] The outstanding eurozone government debt is approximately €4.8 trillion, compared to $4.3 trillion in the US.

[57] See Pierron (2004).

[58] Assuming 255 open market days per year. Following an established convention used by the BIS, in the absence of annual turnover figures, daily turnover is multiplied by 255, an approximation for the number of days in a year on which markets are open (see McCauley, 1999, p. 14).

comparison to electronic trading, it remains the minority trading channel for Euro government debt, in particular in the inter-dealer market.

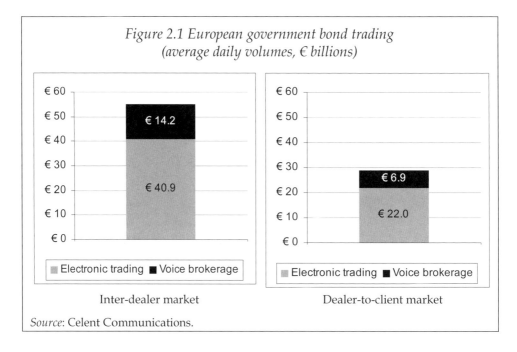

Figure 2.1 European government bond trading (average daily volumes, € billions)

Inter-dealer market | Dealer-to-client market

Source: Celent Communications.

Trading in non-government debt securities in Europe remains substantially below the trading volumes realised in the sovereign market: the total value of sovereign debt trading in the EU is nearly treble the €30.8 billion traded daily in corporate and other debt securities (see Celent Communications, 2004). Therefore, nearly €116 billion worth of debt instruments is traded in the EU every day. If these figures are reliable and if one can extrapolate them over a year, annual turnover in European debt markets today is equivalent to roughly €29.6 trillion.[59] In other words, trading volumes in the EU are about one-third those in US debt markets, where the total US annual trading volume for fixed income is $88 trillion (see Joys, 2001). One could interpret these figures as possibly indicative that US fixed income markets are still considerably more liquid than their

---

[59] Again, daily turnover is multiplied by 255, an approximation for the number of days in a year in which markets are open.

European counterparts, particularly as the total stock of debt in the EU is 80% that of the US (€13.5 trillion vs. €16.7 trillion, as of end-2004).[60]

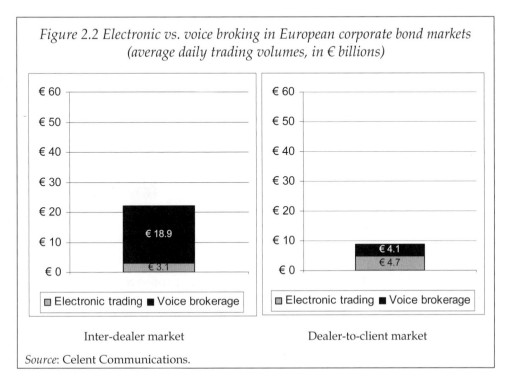

Figure 2.2 Electronic vs. voice broking in European corporate bond markets (average daily trading volumes, in € billions)

Inter-dealer market   Dealer-to-client market

Source: Celent Communications.

As far as the nature of trading is concerned, the B2B inter-dealer market easily surpasses B2C dealer-client transactions in both the sovereign debt and corporate debt segments in the EU, as can be seen in Figures 2.1 and 2.2. In volume terms, inter-dealer trades are more than twice as large as dealer-to-client in the government bond market and more than three times as large in the corporate and other non-government debt segment. B2C transactions on these platforms are purely between dealers and institutional investors; they are not accessible to retail investors (TBMA, 2005a).

That electronic trading dominates voice broking in the government bond segment is not surprising, since this result was to be expected after the introduction of the MTS system and the pressures to concentrate dealer trading on MTS created by the Liquidity Pact. However, other dimensions

---

[60] BIS figures.

of the same market, such as asset swaps, switches (where an older bond is sold simultaneously with the purchase of a new issue of similar maturity) and repo, are traded in a variety of ways: through other electronic systems, voice brokers or directly between the banks. Neither is it astonishing that a larger proportion of dealer-to-client transactions in sovereign bonds are carried out via telephone, as institutional investors have client relationships with a limited number of banks, and this market segment typically functions on a 'request for quote' basis rather than fully interactive bids and offers to the market at large. The institutional investor will therefore request a price to buy or sell from a set of its chosen banks and choose the most favourable terms.

As one can see in Figure 2.2, the great majority of non-government bonds (in volume terms) in the EU are still traded via voice brokerage, as opposed to electronic trading. While it is very likely that the corporate debt segment of the market will remain a hybrid mix of electronic trading and voice broking, the speed of the gains in market share made by electronic platforms is still impressive, given that transactions in the non-government segment of the market were almost exclusively conducted via telephone only a short while ago. For example, in the dealer-to-client segment of the European corporate debt market, electronic trading even surpassed voice brokerage in 2003 according to Celent – although more recently, there has been an upsurge in overall voice-broking in European bond markets. Electronic trading has been slower to catch on in the corporate debt segment, particularly in less-liquid, high-yield issues. Due to their intrinsic illiquidity vis-à-vis actively traded bonds, lower rated bonds, structured products and non-bullet bonds with complex features are not well suited to electronic trading, and the vast majority of transactions in these instruments is still conducted via voice broking (TBMA, 2005a).

As mentioned above, a number of different electronic trading platforms are operational across the EU today. An excellent survey of the existing platforms by The Bond Market Association (2005a) highlights the diversity of electronic trading platforms present in European fixed income markets. The report reaches instructive conclusions about the degree of price transparency prevailing on these various platforms: most platforms publish post-trade prices for trades conducted on their platforms with minimal, if any, delay; post-trade pricing information is provided free of charge to platform participants; some platforms sell data to non-participants (non-vendors) at a fee; most platform trade prices are accessible through a financial data distribution network; and most platforms provide significant non-price information (TBMA, 2004, p. 10).

iv.   Over-the-counter vs. on-exchange bond trading in the EU

It is difficult to tell how much exactly of the secondary market activity in fixed income takes place on-exchange versus in the over-the-counter market, since the latter is diverse and figures are difficult to obtain. However, hardly any trading occurs 'on-exchange' in the wholesale or institutional market, and the only activity is in the retail segment. Bonds are clearly not organised along a model of limit-order markets as equities: in *value* terms, only 2.35% of bond trades in the EU were made via electronic order book transactions in 2004.[61] Evidently, in terms of the total *number* of trades, the electronic order book gains significance, as we shall see below.

In 2004, a total of 10,334,176 bond trades took place on Europe's exchanges (comprising 5,296,106 electronic order book trades plus 5,009,585 negotiated deals).[62] Since it is difficult to obtain figures for the total number of bond trades overall in the EU due to the lack of data for the OTC market, we approximate total bond trades for the EU in 2004 in the following manner: we assumed that the average over-the-counter trade was the same size as the average negotiated on-exchange deal. The average on-exchange negotiated deal in Europe in 2004 was €1.52 million (compared to €129,077 for order book transactions). As mentioned above, the total value of bond trading in the EU is around €114.8 billion a day, which comes out to €29 trillion yearly.[63] If FESE's figures are accurate (so that there is no overlap between their figures reported for on-exchange trades and what really are over-the-counter transactions), then €9.7 trillion in bonds is traded yearly on European exchanges, in which case the value of over-the-counter trades in bonds is €29 trillion – €9.7 trillion = €19.3 trillion. Using our

---

[61] Authors' own calculations using data from FESE, Celent and other authors' calculations. Celent (Pierron, 2004) estimates total bond trading activity in the EU to be €114.8 billion daily. We multiply this figure by 255 to get a yearly figure of €29 trillion. FESE reports the value of electronic order book transactions in bonds in 2004 to be €683.4 billion. Our figure is obtained by dividing the latter by the former.

[62] Based on data from FESE and authors' own calculations.

[63] Again, we calculate yearly figures using the convention of multiplying average daily value of trading by 255.

approximation that the average OTC trade size in bonds is equivalent to the average size of an on-exchange negotiated deal, we estimate that there were 12,732,894 bond trades in the over-the-counter market in 2004. Added to on-exchange trades *assuming no overlap*, there were about 23 million bond trades in the EU in 2004.[64] Since FESE reports 5,296,106 electronic order book transactions for bonds on EU exchanges in 2004, their share in total transactions is very nearly 23%. In other words, almost a quarter of the total number of bond trades in the EU have an average value of €129,077. If our estimates are accurate, the landscape of the European bond market more or less mirrors the US bond market. 'Retail'-sized trades[65] in the US market are large in number (accounting for 65% of total trades), but very small in value terms (1.8%).[66]

In comparison to the secondary market for equities, bond trading in the EU is considerably smaller in terms of total contracts traded, but much larger in notional value and number of securities. Even though our estimate of 23 million bond trades in the EU market last year is likely to be optimistic, at 306 million, total equity trades in the EU in 2004 still were nearly 15 times greater.[67] Yet in terms of the *value* of assets traded, the situation is the reverse: bond trades outdid equities nearly 3:1. Total reported daily turnover on all European stock exchanges combined for the year 2004 was €11.2 trillion.[68] Nevertheless, trading in both the equity and bond markets is dwarfed by the enormous value of transactions in the foreign exchange market, whose daily turnover in the London market alone is about €754 billion, or the equivalent of €192 trillion yearly.[69]

---

[64] Admittedly, the 'no overlap' assumption is highly questionable. There is undoubtedly a high risk of overlap between what exchanges report as on-exchange trades and what truly are over-the-counter trades, meaning that our estimate is probably inflated, because the exchange figures very likely count some transactions as on-exchange activity, whereas they really are over-the-counter transactions that were reported to the exchange.

[65] Evidently, defining a 'retail' trade as anything below $100,000 in value is contentious.

[66] Edwards & Piwowar (2004).

[67] Data from FESE, cumulative for 2004.

[68] Based on data from FESE and authors' own calculations. This compares to our estimate of €29 trillion yearly in European bond markets.

[69] The figure cited on www.thinklondon.com of €754 billion was multiplied by 255 to get an annual turnover estimate.

Beyond aggregate figures, it is interesting to examine differences in on-exchange trading of bonds across EU member states and in other regions of the world. Despite their small size relative to over-the-counter activity and to trading on the MTS system (which is an exchange of 'regulated market' in EU terminology – except for EuroMTS), European national stock exchanges still are the most developed and by far the largest in the world for bond trading. In 2004, the top five exchanges – and six out of the top nine – in terms of bond trading value were all European (see Table 2.2).

Table 2.2 Leading exchanges for bond trading

Exchange	€ billions
1. BME Spanish Exchanges	2856.3
2. London Stock Exchange	2245.3
3. OMX Stockholm	1238.8
4. Copenhagen Stock Exchange	950.2
5. Deutsche Börse	355.3
6. Istanbul Stock Exchange	336.8
7. Korea Stock Exchange	271.7
8. Colombia Stock Exchange	188.9
9. Euronext	186.5
10. National Stock Exchange India	167.2

Note: WFE quotes in US dollars, which were converted to euro at a rate of $1 = €0.8039, the average €/$ exchange rate for 2004, according to the US Internal Revenue Service.

Source: World Federation of Exchanges (WFE) 2004 Annual Report and authors' own calculations.

What is immediately obvious is that a mere handful of exchanges dominate on-exchange trading of bonds in the EU. The four Spanish exchanges alone (dominated by Bolsa de Madrid) account for 29.3% of on-exchange secondary activity in bonds (excluding MTS). Together, the Spanish exchanges, the LSE, OMX, Copenhagen Stock exchange and Deutsche Börse account for nearly 80% (again, excluding MTS).

That the average size of electronic order book transactions for bond trades on EU exchanges is merely a tenth the size of the average negotiated deals seems logical.[70] Electronic order book transactions are typically used

---

[70] In fact, it is almost tautological, since negotiated deals very frequently arise for orders that are too large to introduce all at once into the electronic order book

by retail investors or investors who require immediacy (due perhaps to profitable private information) and who split up large orders into many smaller ones. However, larger trades that result e.g. from institutional portfolio rebalancing or dealer inventory management (liquidity trades) are typically negotiated in 'upstairs trading'. As can be seen in Table 2.3 below, there is a marked variability in the average size of both order book transactions and negotiated deals.

Table 2.3 On-exchange bond trading: Order book vs. deals

	Electronic order book transactions			Negotiated deals		
Exchange	Trades	Turnover (€ millions)	Avg. size , €	Trades	Turnover (€ millions)	Avg. size , €
Borsa Italiana	3,071,806	151,171	49,212	n/a	n/a	n/a
Euronext	1,409,860	19,799	14,043	112,403	166,368	1,480,106
London Stock Exchange	0	0	0	407,102	2,235,843	5,492,096
OMX Copenhagen	25,461	46,099	1,810,557	952,031	902,756	948,243
Bolsa Madrid	29,901	402,137	13,448,948	684,570	2,457,163	3,589,352
Swiss exchange	518,396	35,577	68,628	138,961	102,371	736,686
Total EU	*5,296,106*	*683,604*	*129,077*	*5,009,585*	*7,612,540*	*1,519,595*

Source: FESE 2004 figures and authors' own calculations.

The Italian market is known to have a strong retail component, and after Euronext (€14,043), Borsa Italiana has the smallest average trade size (€49,212) in EU bond order books; on the other hand, the Spanish exchanges stand out with an enormous average trade size of €13.4 million in the electronic order book, which is several times even the average size of negotiated trades. This is perhaps due to the large concentration of government debt trading on the Spanish exchange. In the negotiated deals transactions, it is not surprising that the largest average bond trade sizes are registered on the LSE.

In terms of the breakdown between on-exchange trades in public sector vs. non-public sector bonds in value terms, the former occupies a larger total share in trading (55.6%) compared to the latter (42.7%). The difference is explained by on-exchange trading of international bonds

without moving prices significantly against the trading party bringing forward the request to trade.

(1.7%).[71] The Copenhagen Stock Exchange (and OMX more generally, due to Copenhagen) is the exception to this rule, since 82.4% of bond trading concerns non-public sector securities.[72] Another interesting feature is the small average size of electronic orders for non-public sector bonds on the Italian exchange (€14,305).

2.3 The structure of European bond derivatives markets

i. *Futures and options*

As shown in Table 2.4, fixed income derivatives have grown at a very quick pace in Europe after the introduction of a common currency. Over the period 2000-04, the number of contracts for bond derivatives (options and futures) in the EU grew by an average annual rate of 32.9%, and the corresponding figure for notional value was 36.4% annually.[73] Nominal turnover in bond options has witnessed the most rapid growth of all these categories with annual rates almost reaching 100%. That the options market has been growing faster than futures is not in itself surprising, since options are a sizeably smaller market than futures, reaching only 30% of the futures market in 2004 in terms of nominal turnover and 16% in terms of the total volume of contracts.

Interestingly, most of the growth in fixed income derivatives has been driven by the Liffe market, where total contracts in 2004 is 7.2 times what it was in 2000, and the value of turnover has more than tripled (Table 2.5). Both categories have more or less doubled on Eurex in the same time period.

The market for bond derivatives in the EU is dominated by Eurex, the German-Swiss exchange. Eurex enjoys an almost exclusive market share in some German government debt futures, e.g. 10-year Bunds and shorter-term Bobls (5-year maturity range), having successfully over a 21-month period recaptured back trading activity in this market segment from Liffe, which had a 65% market share in German futures as of 1997) (Pirrong, 2003). In terms of exchange traded bond derivatives, Liffe has retained the

---

[71] Authors' own calculations based on FESE data for the month of December 2004 only.

[72] This is probably due to the very large size of the covered bond market in Denmark.

[73] Authors' own calculations based on data from Table 2.4.

long gilt[74] futures and options, but it also offers Schatz and Bund futures,[75] Bund options and Japanese government futures.

Table 2.4 European bond derivatives' explosive growth

		2000	2004	Growth in %, 2000-04
Bond options	Contracts	30,381,359	127,681,324	320.3
	Notional turnover (€ millions)	14,847,514.4	77,700,713	423.3
Bond futures	Contracts	308,066,560	766,287,667	148.7
	Notional turnover (€ millions)	106,850,300.3	265,520,308	148.5
Total	Contracts	338,230,467	893,968,991	164.3
	Notional turnover (€ millions)	121,679,237	343,221,021	182.1

Source: Authors' own calculations from FESE and Euronext data.

Table 2.5 Engines of growth

Derivative Exchange	Total contracts 2000	Total contracts 2004	Total notional turnover, € millions, 2000	Total notional turnover, € millions, 2004
Euronext.Liffe	43,546,371	313,332,048	90,874,843	278,345,872
Eurex	288,185,156	574,090,908	30,052,951	64,875,149

Source: Authors' own calculations from FESE data.

Both Eurex and Liffe are among the most important futures exchanges in the world in terms of the total number of contracts traded. In but a few years, Eurex has become the single largest futures exchange with close to 700 million contracts traded annually, while Liffe ranks fourth (Table 2.6). Clearly, in terms of the number of contracts traded, Eurex lies at the heart of the bond derivatives market in the EU, easily eclipsing even the

---

[74] British government bonds.

[75] Schatz refers to two-year German government Treasury notes and Bund, to ten-year bonds.

next largest rival, the London Liffe market, now subsumed into Euronext as Euronext.Liffe since January 2002. 574 million futures contracts were traded on Eurex in 2004, or more 1.8 times the number of contracts traded on the Liffe exchange.[76]

Table 2.6 Exchange-traded derivatives: Number of contracts traded on biggest markets

2004 Rank	Exchange	2003 volume	2004 volume	% change
1	Eurex	668,650,028	684,630,502	2.40%
2	Chicago mercantile exchange	530,989,007	664,884,607	25.20%
3	Chicago board of trade	373,669,290	489,230,144	30.90%
4	Euronext.liffe	267,822,143	310,673,375	16.00%
5	Mexican derivatives exchange	173,820,944	210,355,031	21.00%
6	Bolsa de mercadorias & futuros	113,895,061	173,533,508	52.40%
7	New York mercantile exchange	111,789,658	133,284,248	19.20%
8	Dalian commodity exchange	74,973,493	88,034,153	17.40%
9	The Tokyo commodity exchange	87,252,219	74,447,426	-14.70%

Note: Volume figures do not include options on futures.

Source: Futures Industry Association.

Conversely, the notional turnover on Liffe (€278.3 trillion for 2004) was 4.3 times larger than Eurex turnover, meaning that the average size of futures contracts on Liffe are considerably larger than those on Eurex: €847,488 and €115,855, respectively.[77] This contrast is due to the nature of the contracts traded on the respective futures exchanges, since the average value of transactions on exchanges specialising in large-size money market contracts such as Liffe and the Chicago Board of Trade is considerably higher than the average value for longer-term futures contracts such as those traded on Eurex (Jeanneau, 2000). Even so, Eurex still finished third among the world's exchanges after the Chicago Board of Trade ($1,324 billion) and Euronext.liffe ($884 billion) in terms of daily notional turnover, as of 2003 (International Financial Services London, 2004).

With the advent of the euro, futures contracts designed specifically for government benchmark issues in EMU countries other than Germany essentially disappeared together with the legacy national currencies. Because of their high liquidity, German government bond futures like the Schatz, Bund and Bobl had effectively become the hedging instrument of

---

[76] German bond futures account for a large percentage of these.

[77] Authors' own calculations from FESE data.

choice for euro-denominated sovereign debt issues. Presently, all three are traded on the Eurex exchange. Eurex enjoys very high liquidity due to the importance of underlying German government securities as the anchor of the European yield curve, and also as a result of the great degree of standardisation in these products (Table 2.7).[78] German government bond futures are the most traded bond derivatives in the world. The total value of OTC cash market in German government securities is estimated at over €20 billion daily.[79] Recently, Eurex decided to wade into the fiercely competitive cash market for German bonds, launching a platform (with 18 market-makers) that will also allow trading in German Jumbo mortgage/state bonds, European corporate bonds and European covered bonds.

Table 2.7 Eurex contract standardisation

Contract standard	Remaining term in years	Trading unit (Contract value)	Minimum issue	Coupon
Euro-Schatz Futures	1.75 - 2.25	€100,000	€5 billion	6% p.a.
Euro-Bobl Futures	4.5 - 5.5	€100,000	€5 billion	6% p.a.
Euro-Bund Futures	8.5 - 10.5	€100,000	€5 billion	6% p.a.
Euro-Buxl Futures	20 - 30.5	€100,000	€5 billion	6% p.a.

Source: Eurex.

Euronext.Liffe enables the trading of highly complex short-term interest rate derivatives and represents the core of hedging strategies in the euro money markets. Notional turnover in short-term interest rate futures exceeded €204 trillion in 2004, compared with only €2.3 trillion in medium- and long-term interest rate futures. After the launch of its three-month Eurodollar futures and options contracts beginning in March 2004, Euronext.Liffe called upon support from a group of designated market-makers to help establish liquidity by ensuring two-way competitive

---

[78] Obviously, contracts are also highly standardised in the Liffe market, where nominal values for trading Schatz futures is £200,000, while it is only £100,000 for Bunds and long gilts.

[79] www.eurex-bonds.com. Figures are valid as of early 2003.

markets in both the futures and the options contracts.[80] Market-making is organised along two overlapping 8.5 hour sessions, where seven liquidity providers will be actively quoting two-way prices at a given time.[81]

A particularity of the microstructure of derivatives markets is that security design and liquidity provision are bundled and decided by the same economic agents (Bartram & Fehle, 2004). That is, futures exchange members determine jointly the characteristics of the options and futures contracts offered such that they only compete along the liquidity-providing dimension. The purpose of this cooperation is to render trading more efficient and voluminous by improving product standardisation, preserving anonymity in the trading process and easing netting arrangements for the clearinghouse that acts as central counterparty to trades (Bartram & Fehle, 2004). Eurex is an electronic order-driven market where several market-makers compete to provide two-way quotes that are matched against incoming orders. In the Euronext.Liffe market, the Liffe CONNECT trading host matches incoming orders in the central order limit book.

ii.   Over the counter interest rate derivatives

The other associated development since the advent of the euro is the huge growth in the volume of interest rate swaps. As well as the significant increases in bond futures and other interest rate and money market products, the development of flexible and negotiable interest rate products has enhanced financial institutions and lenders' risk management and hedging, and allowed borrowers to securitise income and insulate themselves from future interest rate volatility. Consequently the inter-bank market in euro interest rate swaps is now larger in daily turnover than the bond futures market, which itself is larger than the volume of underlying cash bonds. While Eurex trades in excess of €150 billion in Bund futures daily, this includes institutional and retail activity, so the inter-bank segment is likely to be significantly less. However, the daily turnover in euro-denominated swaps is around €130 billion,[82] far overshadowing the market in physical government bonds in the same inter-bank segment.

---

[80] www.euronext.com.

[81] For the three hours in the day that the opening hours of the London and New York stock markets coincide, 14 market-makers will be quoting prices.

[82] BIS (2004) (http://www.bis.org/publ/rpfx05a.pdf).

This pattern of greater volumes shifting away from the physical bond (which after all represents the cost of government borrowing) can be contrasted with the situation in the US. In the US dollar market, US government bonds trade in a higher volume (estimated at $200 million) than the $80 billion of interest rate swaps. This means that the most accurate interest rate curve in the eurozone is generated by OTC activity in the inter-bank space, in the absence of a coherent and homogenous cost of borrowing for the member state governments.

3. Bond Markets and EU Legislation

3.1 EU FSAP legislation and the bond markets

Securities market regulation at EU level is older than one might initially think. The first piece of legislation dates back to 1979 and relates to the conditions for admission of securities to a stock exchange listing. It was followed in the 1980s by legislation regarding the regime for issuers in capital markets and in the 1990s by regulation covering intermediaries. The common deficiency of these rules was, generally speaking, the low degree of minimum harmonisation, which did not allow mutual recognition to work effectively, and the poor enforcement and insufficient cooperation among the authorities. It was a reflection of the low level of development and the high degree of state protection and fragmentation that characterised Europe's capital markets until recently.

The advent of EMU gave rise to a late plan in 1998 to adapt the regulatory framework to allow a truly single European capital market to emerge in the Financial Services Action Plan (FSAP). It was followed by the Lamfalussy report (European Commission, 2001) in February 2001, which adapted the procedures and instituted the structures for securities market regulation in the EU.

This chapter analyses the impact on the bond markets of the new FSAP measures and the directives on prospectuses, transparency, market abuse and markets in financial instruments and assesses the implementing measures that have been adopted or are being discussed. It will first review some issues raised with regard to bond markets and intermediaries in the pre-FSAP regulatory framework. Annex I lists all EU-level legislation related to capital markets regulation.

3.2   The pre-FSAP regulatory framework

Two directives set the basic standards for issuers in capital markets, covering the minimum financial and non-financial information that must be published and providing mutual recognition: i) the 1980 *listing particulars* directive, which covered the information about securities when listing on an organised market (exchange) in the EU, and ii) the 1989 *prospectus* directive, which concerned initial public offerings of securities that are not to be admitted to listing. Both directives formally applied to debt and equity securities – the distinction being based on listed vs. non-listed – although the 1989 directive was in practice designed for the bond markets and carried a specific reference to and definition of *euro-securities*.

The utility of the prospectus directive was principally hampered by the lack of a common definition of public offer and private placement. This was left to the member states, which interpreted it according to their own provisions, without mutual recognition. Only four member states implemented a specific regime for euro-securities, i.e. Eurobonds, which was of course not identical either.

The free provision of services for intermediaries in capital markets with a single licence was established in the 1993 investment services directive (ISD). This directive set minimum requirements for investment firms to provide their services throughout the EU and for exchanges (regulated markets) to offer remote access. Although the ISD had a considerable impact on the markets, it was judged inadequate as a means of integrating markets and protecting the official market. In particular, conduct of business rules were left to the member state where the service is provided, transparency provisions were found insufficient, and the rules did not apply to multilateral trading facilities (Levin, 2003, pp. 2-5).

3.3   The FSAP measures

The Financial Services Action Plan (FSAP) contains four measures that have a direct impact on bond markets: the prospectus, market abuse, markets in financial instruments and transparency directives. These initiatives replace previous EU measures in these areas. Another element of the FSAP, the International Accounting Standards (IAS) regulation, is also critically important, because it requires listed issuers to adopt IAS. The FSAP measures are closely linked with the Lamfalussy approach, which allows secondary legislation to be agreed upon by a Committee of experts, based on proposals by the Committee of European Securities Regulators (CESR).

i.   The prospectus directive

The new prospectus directive allows firms to organise European-wide, capital-raising exercises on the basis of a single document. A common position was reached on the amended proposal on 5 November 2002, after a first draft had provoked much controversy and final agreement on the text was reached on 7 July 2003. The new regime is composed of three segments: one for equity issuers and non-equity issues below €1,000, a second for non-equity issues with a denomination of at least €1,000, and a third for professional investors.

The key features of the new regime are:

1.   The definition of 'public offer' and 'private placement' at EU level.

2.   The introduction of an enhanced disclosure standard, based on the IOSCO model, in the form of harmonised requirements for debt and equity securities. Accounts need to be prepared on the basis of IFRS or local GAAP if 'equivalent' to IFRS.

3.   The introduction of a new prospectus system composed of a single document or a tripartite of documents. Both forms need to contain the same information, but this distinction was made to speed up approval of the prospectus, which should go faster with a split document. Issuers will thus be allowed to refer to other parts of an approved prospectus (incorporation by reference). The tripartite document needs to be composed of 1) the basic *registration document*, or shelf filing, containing the general information about the issuer and its financial statements, which is to be updated each year; 2) the *securities note*, containing the details about the securities offered to the public and/or for listing and the modalities of the operation; and 3) the *summary note*, containing the main items of both. For offerings under a programme (multiple issues), a single *base prospectus* applies, containing all relevant information (as the registration document), leaving the issuer to refer to the remaining details when making a particular issue.

4.   The possibility to offer securities cross-border on the basis of *a simple and straightforward notification procedure* to host country authorities, and the concentration of supervisory responsibilities in a single home administrative authority. Equity issuers and non-equity issuers below

€1,000 need to have the prospectus vetted in their home country, that is, the country where the issuer has its registered office. For non-equity issues with a denomination of at least €1,000 (or the equivalent in another currency) and for issues for professionals, there will be free choice of the home country of approval of the prospectus. Strict time limits apply by which the home country has to approve a prospectus, or make comments known to the issuer.

5.   For *non-equity* securities traded by professionals, special rules apply. In that case, there will be no obligation to provide a summary and an annual update, to have the prospectus approved in the home country, to have IAS equivalence, etc. The minimum denomination for such securities is €50,000. Other exemptions from the directive are the issue of securities already listed, continuous offerings by credit institutions, issues with a total value of less than €2.5 million and offers addressed to less than 100 persons.

6.   The *maximum harmonisation approach* should allow that one single standard applies throughout the EU. Member states cannot set additional requirements for issuers based in their jurisdictions. The implementing measures were issued as a regulation under EU law, meaning they are directly applicable and do not need to be transposed in national law.

7.   The introduction of a *new language regime*. Only the summary will have to be translated for cross-border offerings in case the prospectus is (also) published in a language that is "customary in the sphere of finance".

In the first draft of May 2001, only one prospectus format was proposed, composed of the set of three documents, without the possibility of choosing the country of approval of the prospectus. This led issuers to complain that the regime would become too onerous and costly. It was furthermore argued that the draft was drawn up primarily with equities in mind, without sufficiently taking into account the specificities of bonds, in particular the eurobonds market. The directive as finally approved takes this criticism into account. It gives almost free choice of regime for bond issuers, but almost no choice for equity issuers. Hence, although the first draft had disregarded the bond markets, this was largely taken into account in the amended Commission proposal, the Council common position and Parliament's second reading.

Following the Lamfalussy approach, implementing measures on the draft directive were adopted by the European Securities Committee on 29 April 2004. It covers the format, minimum information requirements, methods of publication and dissemination and the modalities of incorporation by reference.

Overall, there are no clear views yet on the impact of the new directive on the markets. Initial data do not seem to indicate an abrupt stop in bond issuance after 1 July 2005. On the contrary, the strong growth in European bond markets observed over the last years can be expected to continue. Most observers agree that the new directive should create a truly single passport for issuers, but there are concerns that it may have a negative impact on some segments of the bond markets in Europe, particularly for non-EU issuers, because of the IFRS equivalence requirement. The specific adaptations that have been made for the bond markets, with the special regime for the €50,000 + segment and the free choice of home country for €1,000 + bonds, are welcomed, but are seen as probably still too constraining. On the other hand, incorporation by reference did not exist before and should reduce the cost of issuance. It should also be remarked that the new EU regime is more liberal than that in the US, which simply allowed no choice of home country. Foreign issuers need to follow US rules for issues within the US territory, as is also the case for US issuers.

In the discussion of the possible negative impact of the directive, more reference is made to the competitive threat posed by other jurisdictions, in particular Switzerland and Singapore. The former country introduced a new listing regime for bonds, which came into force on 1 February 2005. Apart from the local standard and IFRS, the new Swiss regime also accepts US GAAP and those of the industrialised countries, and some NICs, such as Brazil and South Africa. Moreover, no distinction is made between the retail and the wholesale regime, i.e. denominations of €1,000 fall in the wholesale regime, and it is not necessary to submit semi-annual financial statements, as is required under the transparency directive, discussed below.[83]

In addition, EU financial centres are reacting as well and creating alternative regimes. The London Stock Exchange (LSE) started the

---

[83] First listing of an international bond under SWX's new additional rules, 29 March 2005 (www.swx.com).

Professional Securities Market, which is regulated by the exchange, but is not a regulated market as defined by the directive. By following this route to listing, issuers will be able to issue any type of debt security or depository receipts, according to LSE.[84] Luxembourg and Dublin are taking similar initiatives to try to pre-empt any possible negative impact of the prospectus directive.

ii.   The transparency directive

Closely linked to the new prospectus regime is the so-called draft transparency directive which updates the modalities for periodic and ad-hoc disclosure of issuers on capital markets. The legislation proposes to integrate all relevant requirements of EU law into a single text, broaden the scope of securities covered so far and upgrade the current regular reporting requirements, following International Financial Reporting Standards (IFRS). However, periodic and ad-hoc disclosure also covers non-financial information, which is related to different company law or corporate governance requirements, and represents a new stream of EU initiatives, which is briefly discussed below.

The requirements of the transparency directive are as follows:

1.   A full *annual financial report* should be published by issuers within four months of the end of the fiscal year and should not only contain the audited financial statements, but also a management report.

2.   A full *semi-annual financial report* should be published by issuers within two months, containing a condensed set of financial statements and an interim management report. This report does not need to be audited.

3.   *Interim management statements* shall be made 10 weeks after the beginning and 6 weeks before the end of each 6-month period. It shall contain an explanation of material events that have taken place during the relevant period and a general description of the financial position and performance of the issuer. Issuers exclusively of debt securities with a denomination of at least €50,000 or equivalent are exempted from these periodic reporting requirements.

---

[84] Professional Securities Market, London Stock Exchange. The Professional Securities Market will be operated and approved as a Multilateral Trading Facility (MTF), as defined by the MiFID (see below). It became operational on 1 July 2005.

4. For the definition of *price-sensitive information*, reference is made to the text contained in the market abuse directive (Art. 6, see heading below).

5. As regards *information dissemination*, the directive requires equal treatment of all security holders. Member state authorities shall ensure there is at least one officially appointed mechanism for the central storage of regulated information. Electronic information dissemination is permitted. It shall require "the issuer to use such media as may reasonably be relied upon for effective dissemination of information to the public throughout its territory and abroad" (Art. 21.1).

6. *Organised dissemination systems.* The directive insists on setting guidelines for the dissemination of regulated information and information provision, but leaves practical arrangements to implementing legislation (level 2) and guidelines to be agreed among member states in the context of the Committee of European Securities Regulators.

7. *Language regime.* The same language regime applies as in the prospectus directive, i.e. the home member state language and one international language (with the exception that there is no summary, which needs to be translated in all cases in the host country language). For large issues (in excess of €50,000), only one language is required.

The requirements regarding periodic disclosure do not apply to state, regional and local authorities, international multilateral bodies or central banks. In the draft implementing measures, CESR has made proposals on minimum information for half-yearly financial statement and published its thoughts on how a single access point may be developed for EU investors to obtain financial information on EU issuers.

iii. Market abuse and insider dealing

A new directive updates the current insider trading directive and adds new provisions on market manipulation, on which no harmonised rules existed before, and which is new for many EU member states. The aims of the directive are to avoid loopholes in Community legislation that would undermine confidence in securities markets. The directive was formally adopted on 3 December 2002. The European Commission, following the proposals by the Committee of European Securities Regulators, has in the meantime adopted implementing legislation regarding several articles of the directive. In the context of disclosure, the most important ones are those relating to the definition of price-sensitive information (Arts. 1 and 6.1 and 6.2) and investment research (Art. 6.5).[85]

- *Inside information* is defined as "information of a precise nature which has not been made public (…) and which, if it were made public, would be likely to have a significant effect on the prices of those financial instruments". This is also the definition that is used for ad-hoc disclosure. In the implementing proposals, this is further defined as "ex-ante available information an average person would be likely to use as part of the basis of his investment decisions in order to optimise his interests".

- Market manipulation is defined as "transactions or orders to trade which give, or are likely to give, false or misleading signals as to the supply of, demand for or price of financial instruments".

- The directive requests member states to ensure that issuers of financial instruments *inform the public as soon as possible* of inside information. This information should be posted on the internet sites of the issuers (Art. 6.1). Delays must be justified to the authorities (Art. 6.2). Disclosure of information to third parties must be complete and effective, and simultaneous for international disclosure (Art. 6.3).

- *Dealings by directors* in shares or options must be notified to the competent authorities. Member states shall ensure public access to information concerning such transactions (Art. 6.4).

- *Investment research* and recommendations must be fairly represented, and factors that are likely to impair its objectivity must be disclosed (Art. 6.5). In the implementing legislation, it is proposed that member states make sure that effective organisational arrangements are in place to prevent conflicts of interest in investment firms; that material conflicts of interest are disclosed and that an overview of all 'buy', 'hold' and 'sell' recommendations is published on a quarterly basis.

- *Single supervisory authority*. Member states must centralise the supervision of market abuse and insider dealing into one single administrative authority (Art. 11). This requires significant changes in

---

[85] Working documents on the implementation of Arts. 1 and 6, paras. 1 and 2 and Art. 6 para. 5 of the European Parliament and Council Directive 2003/6/EC, ESC 12/2003 and 13/2003.

some member states, where first-line supervision is carried out by the stock exchange, or through code of conduct arrangements.

An important issue, which is raised in the implementing legislation, is the synchronisation of inside information disclosure in all member states to guarantee equal treatment of investors. The question how this will be done is left to the member states (level 3) or to implementing legislation. The directive was already effectively applied in several member states.

Table 3.1 Reporting requirements for issuers with listed securities in the prospectus, market abuse and transparency directives

Scope	Prospectus	Market abuse	Transparency
Disclosure regime/ trigger	Initial	Inside information Dealings by directors Conflicts of interest in investment research	Ad-hoc (price-sensitive information, change in major holdings) Periodic (annual, bi-annual and 'quarterly' management reports)
Frequency	Annual updates of all relevant information by issuer	As soon as possible	Max. 3-month delay for annual, 2 months for bi-annual, interim management reports in between No delay for ad-hoc Max. 5 days for changes in major holdings
Dissemination	Issuer's website Press Home authority website	Company website	Issuer's website Member states must ensure timely access
Language regime	Home plus international language or host-country language Summary note must always be translated	(not discussed)	Home plus international language or host country language Single language for issues > €50,000
Exemptions	Lighter regime for issues > €50,000	Monetary policy and Treasury authorities	No periodic reporting requirement for debt securities > €50,000
Degree of comitology	11 of 33 articles	2 of 22 articles	12 of 35 articles

Competent authority	Home country for approval of equity issues Choice for approval of bond issues > €1,000	(not discussed)	Home country or country of choice of issuer
Supervisory authority	Fully independent (with transitory period) Delegation of dissemination authorised	Fully independent	Fully independent Delegation authorised, but subject to caveats, and for a maximum period of 5 years after entry into force
Form of harmonisation	Maximum	Minimum	Minimum
Implementation deadline	1 July 2005	October 2004	January 2007

iv. Markets in financial instruments directive (MiFID)

The cornerstone of the FSAP, the MiFID, sets the rules for intermediaries in EU capital markets. The aim of the new directive is to better protect investors and preserve market integrity while promoting efficient and liquid markets. The directive retains the division between regulated markets and investment firms of the 1993 investment services directive (ISD), which it replaces.[86]

The new MiFID aims to create a coherent, if differentiated, pre- and post-trade transparency regime for regulated markets, multilateral trading facilities (MTFs) and investment firms, which, at this stage, only applies to equity transactions. The MiFID contains stronger rules regarding the operation of investment firms (e.g. conflicts of interest) and their relations with clients (e.g. conduct of business rules). Unlike the ISD, it applies also to investment advice. It introduces for the first time explicit best-execution rules and order-handling rules. For regulated markets, the directive provides for more harmonised rules regarding organisational requirements, admission of instruments to trading and transparency requirements.

Following lengthy consultations within the framework of CESR, the multilateral trading facilities (MTFs), comprising ATSs and crossing-systems, are included in the scope of the directive. This is in line with a functional theory of regulation, which stipulates that the functional

---

[86] This part is updated from Levin (2003).

characteristics and not the institutional form should determine regulatory rights and obligations. Accordingly, the directive imposes similar obligations on MTFs as on regulated markets (e.g. transparency and capital requirements).

The main elements of the new regime are as follows:

- *The transparency regime (applicable to equity instruments only):*
  - ○ *Exchanges.* The directive contains a more comprehensive pre- and post-trade transparency regime. As for *pre-trade information*, Art. 44.1 requires regulated markets to "make public current bid and offer prices which are advertised through their systems for shares admitted to trading". It provides a waiver for large transactions (Art. 44.2). Regarding *post-trade transparency*, regulated markets will have to publish prices, volumes and times of all equity trades at all times on a "reasonable commercial basis" and "as close to real-time as possible" (Art. 45.1). Deferred publication is allowed for large-scale transactions (Art. 45.2).
  - ○ *Multilateral trading facilities (Arts. 29 and 30).* MTFs resemble regulated markets in the sense that they provide a trading facility where users can meet. The MiFID accordingly imposes transparency obligations on MTFs similar to those imposed on regulated markets.
  - ○ *Investment firms (Art. 27).* Systemic internalisers need to publish quotes on a continuous basis for blue chip shares. This provision shall not apply for trades above market size. Volumes and prices of executed trades shall be published as soon as possible. The *client limit-order display rule* (Art. 22.2) requires investment firms to publish those limit orders (instructions to trade at best price, but not below a specified limit) that they cannot execute immediately. The aim is to ensure that the information content of these orders reaches the market. Exceptions are made for large transactions.

- *Best Execution*

  Although it was not called for in the 1993 ISD, EU rules in the future will also contain provisions on best execution. Art. 21 provides that investment firms should execute client orders in such a way that the client obtains the "best possible result" in terms of price, costs, speed, likelihood of execution and settlement, size and nature (Art. 19.1). This execution policy needs to be reviewed on a regular basis. If orders are executed outside the regulated market or an MTF, the investment firm needs to obtain express prior consent of their clients (Art. 19.3). These provisions apply to all financial instruments including bonds.

The broader conduct of business rules (Art. 19) are also aimed at boosting execution quality. Paragraph 3 provides that clients shall receive information on e.g. different execution venues, the costs and associated charges. Art. 25 provides that investment firms must maintain records for all transactions they have carried out on behalf of clients.

- *Conduct of business rules (Art. 19)*

  The MiFID considerably extends the 1993 provisions on conduct of business. The old ISD rules were vague and left significant discretion to the member states (Art. 11). Notably, there was significant ambiguity whether the home or the host country rules were applicable. Moreover, the rules were badly enforced.

  The new rules require firms to act honestly, fairly and professionally in accordance with the best interest of their client, on the basis of some general principles. These will be further worked out by CESR, taking into account the nature of the service, the type of investment service and the character of the investor (retail, professional).

- *Provisions on conflicts of interest (Art. 18)*

  Unlike the ISD, the MiFID contains a self-standing provision on conflicts of interest. It requires investment firms to identify conflicts of interest between themselves and their clients or between clients with conflicting interests (Art. 18.1). Investment firms are required to have arrangements in place to manage those conflicts and prevent them from affecting their clients' interests. If such arrangements are not enough to prevent conflicts, investment firms must disclose the source and nature of the conflict to potential clients before undertaking any business (Art. 18.2).

- *MiFID and the bond markets*

  Art. 65.1 requires the European Commission to submit a review to the European Parliament "on the possible extension of the pre- and post-trade transparency provisions to the transactions in classes of financial instruments other than shares". A recent draft of the European Parliament (2005) report (Rapporteur: Ieke van der Burg) asked the Commission to focus on "possible problems in bond trading, and invited the Commission to bring forward proposals related to bond markets under Art. 65.1 of the MiFID on the basis of an analysis of any problems that it identifies concerning price transparency in bond trading in the European Union" (paragraph 23).[87] Although this wording was not maintained in the final report and replaced by a very vague reference, it remains indicative of the policy pressures that are building up regarding this subject.

As with the ISD, the MiFID does not apply to primary government-debt markets. The organisation of these markets is left to the discretion of the member states. However, some standardisation has been occurring in that market and governments have, in the context of the Economic and Financial Committee, agreed on a new harmonised format for primary dealers to report on their activities in euro-denominated government bonds. Instead of submitting as many as 11 different reports, as in the current system, primary dealers will only be required to provide a single report that combines elements from all eurozone countries. The data provided are one of the key inputs used by the Treasuries to monitor the quality of the primary dealers' contribution to the placement of their securities and to the liquidity of the secondary market. In the new format – applicable from 2006 onwards – primary dealers will provide details on the type of securities traded and the type and geographical location of the counterpart.[88] This however does not address the issues that face the bond market if it becomes mandatory for dealers to publish pre-trade bids and offers real-time.

- *The US NMS rule*

  Unlike EU best execution rules, which require firms to take into account more than only the price, the new Regulation NMS of the US Securities and Exchange Commission requires orders for stocks listed on the NYSE and other regulated markets to be sent to the market that has the best posted price. The rule prohibits bypassing, or 'trading-through' another market's quote for both exchange-listed and Nasdaq securities. It prevents electronic market centres (ECNs) from competing with the

---

[87] The initial draft of the Van der Burg report (Paragraph 23) asked the Commission to focus on "possible problems with access to and transparency in bond trading in the European Union, which is much larger than the European equity market but is reputed to be less efficient than the bond trading market in the USA".

[88] Economic and Financial Committee, Subcommittee on EU Government Bond and Bills Markets, Brussels, 7 April 2005.

NYSE for trading interest. The SEC believes that the uniform trade-through rule would encourage the use of limit orders, aggressive quoting and order interaction and help preserve investors' expectations that their orders will be executed at the best displayed price.

v.   Consolidated accounts in IAS or equivalent

From 2005 onwards, all listed issuers are requested to prepare consolidated accounts in accordance with IAS, or equivalent. This requirement caused much uproar in the markets, as it was feared that the US would never recognise IAS as equivalent, but also since other accounting standards, such as the Japanese, would not meet the test. On 20 April 2005, however, the EU and the US agreed on a roadmap to eliminate from 2007 onwards the SEC requirement for foreign private issuers to reconcile financial statements prepared under IAS to US GAAP, thereby removing a final big hurdle to the development of European capital markets. Nevertheless, the SEC agreement remains conditional on the finding by the SEC staff that IAS financial statements and the accompanying reconciliations are faithful to and consistent with the US GAAP.

vi.   Conclusion

Although many concerns were initially expressed on the negative impact of the new regulatory framework on non-equity markets and on European capital markets in general, it seems that amendments and compromises to draft texts cater for different segments of the markets. The special regime for the €50,000 + segment and the free choice of home country for bonds in excess of €1,000 in the prospectus directive are important concessions to the bond markets, allowing the EU bond market to remain attractive for special segments, and installing a competitive environment between jurisdictions, which does not exist in the US. The IAS equivalence agreement can be considered as a final breakthrough for the EU bond markets.

The main concerns that can be expressed regard the regulatory regime for investment firms. The best execution and conduct of business rules have become onerous for firms to internalise, and may weigh upon market development and innovation. The delay in the implementation of the MiFID should give firms more time to cope with these requirements.[89]

---

[89] According to a Commission press release of 20 June 2005, the Commission proposed to extend the implementation deadline by 6 months, until 30 October

The work to make the single capital market function effectively is now in the hands of the supervisors. Initial evidence on the implementation of the new directives shows that much remains to be done. The latest transposition statistics show an old bad habit has not yet disappeared: notwithstanding the Lamfalussy procedure and the instalment of the 'level 3' Committees, most member states have not managed to have the directive implemented in national law within the time foreseen. This was also the case with the two directives discussed above, which had to be implemented at the time of writing this report, the market abuse and prospectus directives. On the other hand, the increased cooperation between supervisors and the higher scope for secondary legislation than had previously been the case should allow for more consistency in the application of the rules across the member states.

2006. The proposal also gives firms and markets another six months (until 30 April 2007) to adapt their structures and procedures to the new requirements.

4. Bond Market Liquidity, Efficiency and Transparency: The Role of Public Policy

4.1 Introduction

This chapter analyses the role of public policy in contributing to and enhancing bond market liquidity and efficiency. In a first section (4.2), we review why bond markets occupy a vital function in the economy, detailing the various ways in which they contribute to economic growth. This section serves to highlight the importance of enlightened policy-making in the form of targeted and constrained interventions, so as to harness the benefits of wide, deep and resilient bond markets. The next section explains the context in which the MiFID Art. 65 review will take place and sets out guiding principles for regulators to follow when deciding whether to impose new statutory rules on market players or extend existing rules, and highlights the differences between stock and bond markets in terms of the objectives of market participants. It analyses why market rules designed for stock markets are not optimal in the fixed income business. Section 4.4 reviews the importance of liquidity and its contribution to market efficiency, since the debate surrounding MiFID Art. 65 seems to be swirling especially fast around the liquidity-transparency nexus, and examines the question of price transparency against an existing transatlantic benchmark. A final chapter presents a set of recommendations based on conclusions drawn from the present chapter.

4.2 Economic growth and the benefits of dynamic bond markets

i. Introduction

Abundant research [e.g. Levine (2004), Beck, et al. (1999a), Levine, et al. (1999) Levine & Zervos (1999) and Edison, et al. (2002)] has documented how developed, liquid and integrated markets contribute to economic growth by facilitating the efficient allocation of scarce economic resources and risk across space, time, and states of nature. Once it has been established that developed and properly functioning financial markets power the engine of growth in a capitalist economy, it is logical to examine what role bond markets play more specifically. Surprisingly, the research on finance and growth has, until very recently at least, focused almost entirely either on stock markets and banks, or on financial markets more generally, to the exclusion of bond markets. Recently, however, this lacuna has been addressed in the emerging literature on the importance of bond markets for economic growth (see e.g. Herring & Chatusripitak, 2001, or Fink, et al., 2003).

Financial market integration also promotes the efficiency of the financial sector, since a number of financial activities display economies of scale and benefit from the pro-competitive environment of open (economic) borders (European Commission, 2002). There are a number of reasons why the further integration of bond markets would specifically contribute to greater economic efficiency in Europe.[90] These include: greater competition between issuers due to the greater supply of similar (or homogeneous) securities across borders (Pagano & von Thadden, 2004), between intermediaries that translate into lower transaction costs, relaxation of national investment restrictions for pension funds and insurance companies that allows for greater portfolio diversification and correspondingly higher risk-adjusted returns, more accessibility to external sources of finance, better hedging opportunities, and the higher rates of innovation that prevail in large, open markets. In the following paragraphs, we briefly summarise the vital functions fulfilled by bond markets in the economy.

---

[90] European bond markets are known to be significantly more integrated than their equity counterparts. This is particularly true in the sovereign debt segment. Jean-Claude Trichet, President of the European Central Bank, put it this way in a recent speech: "As a broad assessment of the level of integration in the wholesale markets, I would say that it is almost perfect in the money market, including its related interest rate derivatives markets, very well advanced in the government bond market, fairly high in the corporate bond market, and least advanced, but increasing, in the equity market. (BIS, 2005).

ii. *Funding*

(Primary) bond markets contribute to economic dynamism first and foremost by relaxing the constraints that impede firms' access to external funds. In the absence of deep and well-functioning financial markets, profitable investment opportunities identified by managers as such often cannot be exploited: the pool of capital needed to translate growth potential into profits is constrained by the availability of cash reserves (retained earnings) or by relationship ties that bind corporate treasurers to their usual bank lenders. Well-functioning primary markets create the possibility for governments, corporates and financial institutions to raise debt finance. A bond amounts to an inter-temporal contract between an agent holding a surplus of cash today (the investor) and one who faces a cash shortage (the issuer). The investor lends cash to the issuer in exchange for a steady (usually annual or bi-annual) stream of cash flows (coupons or interest payments).[91] If there is a surplus of projects yielding positive net present values today relative to available cash, borrowing enables firms to profitably mobilise future capital today. In turn, profits deriving from this investment are used to pay off the debt with interest at a defined date in the future. This exchange of cash across time facilitates inter-temporal consumption for the investor, and inter-temporal investment for the issuer, leading to a higher effective rate of utilisation of existing capital (which, in a dynamic context, effectively creates new capital). The result is that the economy becomes dynamically more efficient and grows.

Bank lending can, broadly speaking, provide the same welfare gains described above by allowing firms to finance investments in excess of their internal financing capabilities. Yet the primary advantages of issuing securities over borrowing from banks are the diversification of funding sources and the competition for underwriting and placement an issuer can stir up among primary dealers and investors to obtain the most favourable borrowing terms possible. Evidently, the scope for such competition as well as for funding diversification is seriously constrained in the case of relationship banking.[92] While the size of banks loans are limited to the

---

[91] This is the case of a plain-vanilla bond. Obviously, there are a number of other types of bonds that do not match these characteristics, for example, variable rate coupons, convertibles, etc.

[92] Although admittedly, a long-term relationship with a single bank could lead to favourable lending terms for a reliable client.

corporate bank's lending capabilities, the funds that can be raised on the international capital market are virtually unlimited (in normal circumstances) so long as the issuer is deemed sufficiently liquid and creditworthy as the debt burden increases.

Secondary debt markets provide mechanisms for the efficient pricing and management of that debt. In addition, they facilitate the pricing of risk by creating reference (benchmark) rates. They also enable investors to hedge risk. Yields on long-term bonds proxy inflationary expectations by market participants, thereby providing information to central banks that is essential in implementing effective monetary policy decisions. Finally, money market instruments can contribute to a stable and efficient payments system by acting as collateral. More broadly, efficient secondary markets for debt securities fulfil important public functions by contributing significantly to both financial stability and liquidity, quasi-public goods that foster financial development and economic growth. But the relationship between developed bond markets and economic growth goes much deeper yet than only the funding channel, as dynamic debt securities markets impact positively on monetary policy, hedging strategies, financial stability, portfolio and liability management.

iii. Monetary policy

Bond markets play a key role in the implementation of monetary policy. Because of their forward-looking nature, they provide central bankers with important information on the inflationary expectations (and by extension, on the interest rate expectations) of market participants, as reflected in the spreads of longer-dated government bonds over money market instruments. Bond derivatives markets in turn provide useful information on the degree of uncertainty regarding future interest rate movements (Issing, 2002). The comprehensive nature of market data and the fact that, unlike surveys of market participants, they actually reflect real economic decisions, renders them invaluable to central bankers. The efficiency of bonds, bond derivatives and swap markets reinforces the quality of information available to monetary authorities, thereby enabling the latter to better calibrate market responses to changes in interest rates; it also enables them to better communicate the central bank's strategy to the markets, thereby reducing uncertainty in the market, and with it, volatility. As a result of both these informational effects, efficient and developed bond markets foster a more stable and accurate monetary policy stance, with positive results for economic growth.

iv.   Pricing and hedging

Secondary debt markets provide mechanisms for the efficient pricing of private and public issues. This function of price discovery is particularly important in liquid markets for heavily-traded debt securities, such as supranationals, government bonds and AAA-rated quasi-government and corporate issues. Government securities have traditionally been viewed as reliable hedging instruments against interest rate risk and have long represented a benchmark against which non-government securities are priced. Certain attributes of government bonds render them particularly well-suited to these functions, including: low liquidity premiums (because they are so heavily traded), negligible probability of default and well-developed market structure, complete with supporting repo and derivatives markets (IMF, 2001, Chapter 4). As we have seen, however, this is less true of the eurozone, particularly when contrasted with the position in the US.

Bond markets facilitate the pricing of risk across asset markets by creating risk-free benchmark yields along a spectrum of maturities (yield curve). Real returns on benchmark government issues represent the anchor of risk pricing along the yield curve. In turn, these risk-free rates represent the backbone of discount rates used to calculate present values for assets and investment projects alike. Today, in some market segments, interest rate swaps have now overtaken government bonds as the standard benchmarks.[93] According to Batten et al. (2004), European fixed income markets were the first to move away from the traditional approach of referencing government yields as benchmarks, shifting instead to greater use of interest rate swaps. This phenomenon occurred as a result of the absence of a coherent euro benchmark curve based on government securities.

Dynamic bond markets also enable investors to better manage and to hedge risk. Financial institutions in particular make extensive use of government bonds to hedge their considerable exposure to interest rate

---

[93] This phenomenon is not strictly limited to the EU. As the US was successful in consolidating its fiscal deficit in the latter part of the 1990s (to the point where 30-year Treasury bonds were abolished), there was concern among market participants that long-term US benchmark debt would become increasingly illiquid relative to past levels, reducing their attractiveness for hedging purposes. This has led to an increasingly prominent role for swap futures in the US market (see IMF, 2001).

risk, because they are the least risky assets and their yields are highly correlated with yields on private debt (IMF, 2001). For example, as the IMF study indicates, primary dealers who underwrite government issues (e.g. in a bought deal) tend to sell government bonds short, in case the value of their long positions would fall, threatening a capital loss. The development of capital markets is conducive to financial innovation, leading to new instruments such as interest rate options and futures that will create new hedging opportunities and enhance the effectiveness of risk mitigation.

Finally, a vibrant secondary market for debt securities can contribute to a stable and efficient payments system by facilitating the use of collateral. The high liquidity and high degree of standardisation of government benchmark issues make them attractive as collateral, especially those securities on the short end of the yield curve.

v. *Financial cycles and stability*

The development of debt securities markets and market-based financing structures in Europe more generally over the past two decades has changed the role banks play in the financing cycle (Welteke, 2000, p. 2). Financial cycles should become less pronounced as the European economy shifts away from relationship-based banking, because a greater diversification of funding sources, especially by raising funds in the international capital market, provide a certain continuity in the stream of borrowing that may not be matched by the lending patterns of domestic banks during economic downturns. Bond markets disconnect lending activity from domestic credit conditions, smoothing the flow of funds in the case of a credit crunch as domestic financial institutions cut back on lending activities (De Bondt, 2002; Davis, 2001). Because the volatility of credit extended to the private sector diminishes (De Bondt, 2002) with developed debt securities markets, the relationship between real economic activity and financial cycles weakens. As the real economy becomes less dependent on domestic credit conditions, boom-bust investment cycles diminish along with the variability in rates of economic growth, which itself feeds back into a more favourable investment climate (and correspondingly higher growth).

Another drawback of relationship banking is that the political ties that have traditionally been associated with it often amount to a perverse incentive structure. Implicit government guarantees of large banks breed a culture of insufficient accountability of credit portfolio managers, which can undermine financial stability in the long run (Rajan & Zingales, 2002).

vi. Market discipline

Public markets for debt securities contribute to economic efficiency by ensuring that credit allocation decisions are market-driven instead of being influenced by political considerations or cronyism, supported by an infrastructure that is conducive to an environment of greater transparency. As information asymmetries gain importance with the diffusion of debt holdings, greater transparency in financial accounts is necessary (e.g. through more stringent disclosure requirements) along with a large community of financial analysts and respected rating agencies to monitor credit developments (Hakansson, 1998). In the case of relationship banking, the credit risk is concentrated in a single institution, which has intimate knowledge of the borrower's credit standing. Once a firm issues public securities, however, the diffusion of claims held against the issuer leads to a collective action problem of who will intensively monitor credit developments within the firm. Unlike relationship bankers, who accrue detailed information about a borrower over repeated lending programmes, investors buying debt on secondary markets sometimes know very little about the issuer's credit standing. Thus, the combination of asymmetric information and the collective action problem necessitates the creation of independent rating agencies that assess the balance of (credit) risks specific to an issuer. Bond markets exercise a powerful disciplining mechanism in the form of ratings downgrades that punish fiscal profligacy in the case of government issuers and unbridled borrowing in the case of corporate issuers. Investors will react to ratings events and heightened credit risk by demanding higher yields, increasing the cost of funding for issuers.[94]

With respect to sovereign debt issues, bond markets provide the added benefit that they allow public deficits to be financed in a non-inflationary manner when market discipline is effective (European Commission, 2002). By helping to enforce fiscal discipline, secondary markets for debt securities contribute to price stability. Without well-

---

[94] A good recent example in Europe is the announcement by the rating agency Fitch that Italian public finances had suffered a "marked deterioration", prompting the agency to change the rating outlook for Italy from stable to negative. This move suggests a possible downgrade in the near future. Already, S&P lowered Italian sovereign debt from AA+ to AA in 2004, making it the first eurozone country to suffer a downgrade since the introduction of the euro. Following the Fitch announcement, yield spreads of Italian bonds over their German counterparts widened by 1 basis point to about 11 basis points overall (see Chung, 2005).

established markets for government securities, the only available instrument for governments to cover budgetary shortfalls is to print money, which results in the building up of inflationary pressures.[95]

Corporate debt markets also can improve corporate governance and the market for corporate control (De Bondt, 2002, p. 7). They promote the efficiency of the economy by facilitating the conditions for corporate restructuring and liquidation.

vii.   Liability and portfolio management

Well-functioning bond markets provide a useful platform for long-term liability management, particularly for insurance firms and pension funds. In the case of these types of financial activities, where liabilities weigh in at long maturities, it is helpful for portfolio managers to obtain a regular source of fixed income. In the case of highly-rated vanilla bonds, the advantage of such instruments is that (in the absence of inflation) their real (as opposed to nominal) value can be determined very precisely, unlike other types of debt instruments such as convertibles or equities. Portfolio management benefits from liquid bond markets since they offer a very wide range of securities whose returns tend to be correlated, facilitating hedging. On the other hand, debt instruments can generate unique payoff structures that can diversify the sources of income.

viii.   Conclusion

Liquid and efficient bond markets occupy a vital function in the economy. They foster market discipline, reduce the temptation for governments to seek recourse via inflationary financing (and therefore contribute to price stability), promote financial stability by mitigating the effects of the credit cycle and by facilitating hedging activities, offer instruments that are used as a basis upon which to price risk along the yield curve and across all asset classes, increase the opportunities for portfolio diversification and encourage more efficient liability management. More broadly, efficient secondary markets for debt securities fulfil important public functions by

---

[95] Whether or not there is a 1:1 relationship between increases in the money supply and inflation has been the matter of considerable debate among academic economists. The consensus view today is that in the short term, frictions such as money illusion and fixed wages (as opposed to automatically adjusted wages) do not support such a relationship. However, there is virtually unanimity among experts that in the long term, this relationship is a strong one.

contributing in a non-negligible manner to both financial stability and liquidity, quasi-public goods that foster financial development and economic growth.

Because of the important functions bond markets exercise in the economy, it is essential that they be allowed to flourish. At the same time, it is natural for regulators to take an interest in discerning if the existing market architecture and the prevalent self-regulatory model are conducive to efficient, deep, fair and liquid markets.

4.3   Regulating bond markets in Europe

i.   *Why the recent attention on bond markets?*

The shift away from bank lending to corporate debt issuing as a source of funding gives regulators good cause to take a closer and greater interest in bond markets (Langton, 2005). Apart from this natural consequence of the ongoing transformation of European financial markets, the debate in Europe has been motivated by several phenomena: the controversial prospect that equity-type price transparency rules may be applied to bond markets in the context of the MiFID Art. 65.1 review. Second, bond markets, which are far less familiar to the average citizen than stock markets, have recently come under public scrutiny — perhaps unfairly, due to a number of events triggered by questionable, unrelated business practices and outright corporate malfeasance, as in the cases of Parmalat and Ahold. Nevertheless, the string of recent corporate defaults in the EU (very high by historical standards), leads one to wonder to what extent greater transparency would have at least alleviated some investor losses. Indeed, since the year 2000, there have been 41 corporate debt defaults in the EU, and no fewer than 20 in the year 2002 alone (S&P, 2005). By comparison, there were only 7 of them between 1991 and 1999 (S&P, 2005). Finally, although one must note that the Citigroup affair was a case of poor judgment, rather than an issue of transparency per se, it is not unfair to say that in that particular case, the unique structure of cash government bond markets drew public attention, accompanied by regulatory scrutiny in several EU countries.[96] For the first time since the introduction of the euro,

---

[96] Reading the leaked memo that initiated the controversy, however, one discovers that the ultimate objective of Citigroup's fixed income traders on 2 August 2004, was to render the European sovereign debt market less transparent and to have fewer dealers providing liquidity in secondary markets, along the lines of the market for US Treasuries.

questions were asked about how real the market made at the request of member states actually was, and whether primary dealer structures reinforce the fractured shape of eurozone debt markets. In the minds of regulators on both sides of the Atlantic, clamours from distraught investors for "something to be done" justify the new-found public interest in determining whether the existing, predominantly self-regulatory framework governing bond markets is sufficiently aligned with public policy objectives. Naturally, public calls for public authorities to intervene in market activity should not translate automatically into new statutory measures. To begin with, it is likely that such action often results from a failure to properly enforce existing regulations. Second, in line with the European Commission's new regulatory approach, any additional statutory measure should stand the test of a rigorous market failure analysis and, perhaps more importantly, once statutory measures are agreed upon as the most effective way to treat a problem, the degree of regulatory intrusion should be proportional to the associated policy objectives while satisfactorily passing a cost and benefit analysis.

Parallel to these recent events in credit markets, an ongoing and powerful trend, namely, Europe's demographic decline, virtually guarantees that retail investor participation in fixed income markets, although relatively low today, will rise substantially in the coming years. Whereas in 1950, 23.2% of the population was over 50 years, the same age group is projected to reach 44% by 2025 (European Commission, 2004). As they grow older, retail investors become more risk-averse, looking to re-balance their portfolios to a predominantly fixed income composition. When this individual behavioural shift to risk-aversion is aggregated across the European economy, the impact on financial markets will be significant. Since the retail investment community in the EU will be composed mostly of ageing or retired workers within a few years, it is safe to predict that fixed income securities will acquire a greater importance in terms of their relative share in portfolio investments than was the case in the past.

ii.   Principles for bond market regulation

Answering the normative questions 'why regulate bond markets?' and 'how?' has acquired a particular importance today, in light of the emerging public debate and informal EU Commission consultations on whether certain MiFID price transparency prescriptions ought to be applied to bond markets. The expected rise in retail investor participation in bond markets poses a major challenge to regulators to strike the right balance between protecting investors on the one hand and not damaging an infrastructure that has developed out of the wholesale business on the other. It is an issue that is likely to only intensify with time, as retail participation will continue to be propelled by technological developments, the ageing crisis, low returns on interest-bearing deposit accounts (in a climate of continued low inflation) and any continued poor performance by equities, as was the case in recent years. In the United States, where such figures are more readily available than in the EU, retail participation in bond markets grew by 70% between 1995 and 1999.[97]

In very general terms, the key policy objectives with regard to the proper functioning of bond markets include:

- Efficiency
- Liquidity
- Stability
- Fairness
- Transparency
- Competitiveness/market self-determination

It is debatable whether transparency ought to be an objective for market regulators to pursue for its own sake. Arguably, the best way to characterise the objective of transparency is as an intermediate objective and not as an end in itself. That is, one could consider transparency to be desirable only *insofar as* it contributes to market efficiency, liquidity and stability.

During the latter part of the 1990s, however, a consensus emerged among regulators that transparency was a desirable trait for securities markets, leading to a revolution in trade-related disclosure. In fact, the objective of transparency had reached such high priority that it was to be the 'golden rule' of the new international financial system, according to former IMF director Michel Camdessus (1999, p. 3). At the time, debt markets were almost completely in the dark in terms of price transparency.[98] The existing pre-trade price publications customarily made

---

[97] See testimony by Doug Schulman (2004) before the United States Senate Committee on Banking, Housing and Urban Affairs.

[98] The notable exception is in the US, where as discussed above it is the "on-the-run" Treasury bond yield curve that is the benchmark for USD interest rates. In this market pre-trade transparency has an intrinsic commercial value not just for

by brokers were enhanced by the introduction of GovPX in 1991 in the US. For less liquid bonds, post-trade price transparency requirements became the norm and were gradually introduced over time, the best example being the TRACE system implemented in the US in July 2002. Transparency in general is today considered an important property which helps to ensure market quality. In its Objectives and Principles of Securities Regulation, IOSCO (2001) recognises in Principle 27 that "regulation should promote transparency of trading" and lists transparency as one of its three core objectives, along with efficiency and fairness. One could argue that transparency is also a determinant of, and, in some cases, a precondition for fair, stable and efficient markets. In the words of Michel Camdessus (1999, p. 3): "Markets cannot work efficiently, and they will remain vulnerable to instability in the absence of adequate, reliable, and timely information from all quarters." At the same time, there is abundant evidence that transparency, despite a common misconception to the contrary, will not always improve market quality. Thus, the academic literature recognises that there exists an optimum degree of (price) transparency: "Even though understanding of this area is very incomplete, the evidence that there is not a simple, unidirectional relationship between transparency and the quality of markets deserves considerable weight in policy-making" (Allen et al., 2001, p. 40; see also O'Hara, 1995).

Mainly for historical reasons, but also because of the relative absence of any considerable retail investor activity until very recently, secondary corporate bond markets have largely operated outside the scope of government statutory regulation, including in the realm of transparency provisions. Although most bonds are listed on exchanges — Luxembourg and London for the overwhelming majority of international bonds — due to the regulatory restrictions on institutional investment placements (they are often precluded from holding unlisted securities for investor protection reasons), trading in bonds is mostly over the counter (OTC).[99] Given the initial conditions, i.e. that bond markets were (and still are)

---

the purposes of trading but also pricing and other reference benchmarking for other interest rate products.

[99] Exchange listing is often seen as a requirement for widening the investor base and enhancing the acceptability of bonds, particularly when institutional investors are prohibited from holding unlisted securities. The predominance of OTC trading is due to the relative ease of trading because of the absence of minimum trading amounts, less restrictive trading times, and expeditious and prompt settlements.

overwhelmingly driven by wholesale transactions, regulators did not see the need to interfere in the established self-regulatory governance structure – to the extent that bond market activity was not prejudicial to other policy objectives, such as financial stability – as they deemed institutional investors to be sufficiently sophisticated to look after their own interests. Nevertheless, as mentioned above, regulators are curious to assess whether the self-regulatory framework adequately protects certain classes of market participants, such as retail investors. Since concerns for the latter's welfare have received so much attention in both the EU and the US recently, we will suggest a strategy for enhancing their protection in bond markets without necessarily disturbing the transparency equilibrium. Central to any possible regulatory initiative is the importance of highlighting the differences between debt and equity markets – the topic of the next section.

Whatever the outcome of the Art. 65 review, the very successful evolution of European bond markets in an almost exclusively self-regulatory environment over the past few decades imposes a certain responsibility on the part of regulators to proceed slowly and with caution, if and when they deem it necessary to intervene further in the bond market.

iii. Some fundamental differences between stocks, bonds and their respective market microstructures

Bond markets, and fixed income markets in general, differ from equity markets in terms of three broad categories: instruments, investor types and objectives, and market microstructure. Differences between stocks and bonds do not stop at the characteristics of these financing instruments but also include: the type of investor, the trading/holding strategy and a number of variables related to market microstructure, including particularities of market-making, extent of retail investor participation, degree of inter-dealer trading and the price discovery process. These differences are highlighted below.

Instruments

Fixed income securities are much more complicated and varied than equities. Whereas equity issued by a firm is everywhere the same in terms of risk and cash flows, the same cannot be said of debt securities. On the other hand, bonds can be issued in a number of different currencies and maturities, either in the domestic or international market, or a combination of both in the context of a borrowing programme; with fixed rate or floating rates, with or without coupons; callable, puttable or neither; secured or unsecured; senior or junior; convertible or straight. This incredible diversity in financing choices provided by the bond requires a certain degree of sophistication on the part of the investor to fully appreciate and manage the risks that are inherent to this instrument. Default risk is certainly not the only source of risk in a bond. Other sources of risk may or may not include: currency risk, interest rate risk, price movements surrounding a corporate treasury's decision to call a bond, to issue more bonds, to convert a bond, etc., meaning that retail investors may not, contrary perhaps to their expectations, recover the full amount of the principal invested. Some fundamental differences between stocks and bonds are highlighted in Table 4.1.

Table 4.1 Differences between stocks and bonds

	Equities	Bonds
Market microstructure		
Price-discovery	Trades carry significant information about counterparties' knowledge of firms' prospects. Trades are information rich	Trades *can* carry firm-specific information, but much rarer than for equities; mostly price movements respond to macroeconomic developments
Market-making	Market-maker at an informational disadvantage vis-à-vis traders with private information, leading to wider bid-ask spreads	Characterised by fewer information asymmetries, so market-makers are less disadvantaged than in equities.
Inventory management	More active inventory management (It would seem so, since inventory imbalances are not easily rectified by hedging)	More passive. Inventory imbalances can be redressed through hedging strategies, so inventory does not need to be re-balanced continuously
Inter-dealer trading	40% (LSE)[a]	47-60% (for govt. securities); about 60% for corporate bonds
Inter-dealer trading by inter-dealer brokers	40-60% (LSE)[a]	95% (US Treasuries); 98% (UK gilts)[a]

Retail investor participation	Considerable, not only in volume, but also in value terms.	In the US 60% in volume terms, but only 1.8% in value terms.[b] In the EU, our estimates in Chapter 2 reveal a situation that more or less mirrors the one in the US.
Time for counter-parties to respond to quotes posted by a dealer	Almost instantaneous for blue-chip stocks	1-2 minutes for plain vanilla bond; 10 minutes for bonds with complex features, e.g. call/put provisions, sinking funds, etc.; up to one day for illiquid bonds and for transactions > $10 million[c]
Order flow	Continuous, small tickets	Discontinuous, much larger tickets traded
Security		
Maturity	Infinite	Finite (except for UK consoles and other perpetuals). Most maturities < 50 years
Heterogeneity	Single stock; no heterogeneity in the asset's payoff structure: equities are alike	Multiple debt issues per firm, varying in currency of denomination, maturity, and yield
Hedgability	Few instruments available for hedging; suggests that inventory imbalances are best redressed by readjusting inventory	Relatively easy to hedge: numerous comparable instruments improve hedgability; offers greater flexibility for inventory mgt
Liquidity	Depends on stock type: blue chip, mid cap or small cap. Smaller issues are less liquid, but still trade hands frequently relative to most bands; absent market distress, liquidity remains more or less constant over time	Similar pattern of liquidity across all bonds: immediately after issuance, trading is high but eventually the issues make their way to buy and hold investors and subsequently become illiquid; issues more liquid on the run than off the run

Investor		
Type of investor	Retail investors, mutual funds, hedge funds	Dominated by pension and insurance funds; very little retail activity in value terms; more concentrated holdings

[a] Gravelle (2002, p. 16).

[b] Harris (2004) defines a 'retail' transaction as $100,000 or less. The arbitrariness of the cut-off and its large nominal value warrant a cautious interpretation of these figures.

[c] Saunders et al. (2002).

Investors

Institutional investors constitute the cornerstone of the European corporate bond market in both the investment grade and speculative grade segments. While 46% of the European primary market in investment grade debt is accounted for by institutional investors, the corresponding figure is 47% for the high-yield end of the market (see Figures 4.1 below). In both market segments, private clients only account for 4% of total holdings. Hedge funds account for 9% and 23% of holdings in the investment grade and speculative grade markets, respectively. Nevertheless, due to leveraged positions and active trading strategies, they may account for a significantly larger ratio of trading turnover.

Essentially, pension and insurance fund trading strategies will revolve around avoiding or minimising mismatches in the maturities of their assets and liabilities, as opposed to staking speculative positions. Liquid and high credit bonds present lower intrinsic volatility than shares due to having a fixed notional amount and calculable yield. Because their liabilities tend to have long horizons, pension and insurance funds look for assets with long maturities. As 'buy and hold' investors, their bond trading strategies are not very sophisticated and they are not active traders. It is primarily for this reason that liquidity in bond issues recedes very quickly after issuance. Likewise, the trading strategies of individual retail investors are typically 'buy and hold', so as to secure a reliably constant stream of income over time. As more specialised (speculative or hedge) funds enter the market, one could envisage greater liquidity in high-yield debt, for example, than historical data would lead one to expect. In addition, the relaxation of regulatory restrictions on pension and insurance fund operations might encourage institutional investors to take advantage of their new found autonomy to trade more actively in secondary markets.

Figure 4.1. Breakdown of European non-government bond markets by investor type

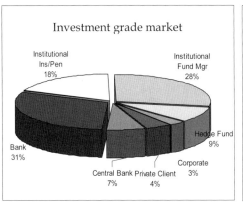

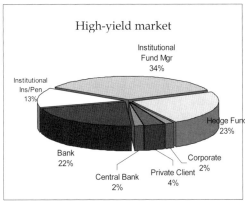

Source: TBMA (2005b).

Market microstructure

One of the single most important differences between stock and bond markets relates to the different underlying price discovery processes. Some generic features of bonds and equities affect the way they are traded on secondary markets and the behaviour of market-makers. Perhaps the most fundamental difference relates to the degree that information asymmetries are present in the trading process, which itself is a result of the huge range and diversity of the bonds' universe. Privileged information about an asset or the flow of orders for an asset is a crucial determinant of trading and market-making decisions, since it allows those who have an informational advantage to act profitably on that information.

But unlike stocks, whose (potential) dividends vary greatly over time, (plain vanilla) bonds yield a predefined cash flow over time. In the case of such bonds, the source of price variability is therefore unrelated (except for the positive probability of default) to variability in the expected cash flow. This property of bonds makes it rather difficult for traders holding private information about a firm to consistently trade profitably in bond markets. Unlike stocks, the value of a bond, default probabilities aside, has less to do with firm-specific characteristics than it does with wider macroeconomic variables, such as contemporaneous and expected interest rate movements. The degree of informational advantages traders can have vis-à-vis counterparties is therefore extremely limited in government debt markets, and more limited in the corporate bond than in equity markets (See

Fleming, 2001). Information asymmetries in the bond market are further reduced by the role of rating agencies and independent opinions they provide on the current likelihood of future default by debt issuers. Determining the price of equity requires far more knowledge about a firm's operations, opening the way for information asymmetries to widen between 'insiders' and 'outsiders'. The way traders interact with each other and with market-makers is therefore fundamentally different in equity and bond markets.

Nevertheless, corporate bonds and especially the high-yield segment do offer opportunities for profitable trading to arise from private information. The risk of default is always present, and it is a variable that is conducive to the formation of private information. But since credit risk does not vary much from day-to-day, the argument that wide spreads are necessary to protect the market-maker against informed traders all the time could seem tenuous: the opportunity of trading profitably on inside information related to the probability of a firm defaulting on its debt being very rare, it cannot represent a regular motivation to trade. Pre-trade transparency is essential in equity markets because equities are traded on a regular basis, and the view of the future performance of the issuer or its sector is inevitably subjective. Unlike bonds, which have a short life, equity securities discount cash flows that are projected *ad infinitum* and can be affected by an array of different variables. Because a host of variables impact stock prices and stock valuation is very sensitive to any new information, the efficient discovery of fair prices requires frequent trading. While other variables such as liquidity also play a role in the determination of bond prices, the fundamental determinant of price really is the credit risk. Yet interest rate movements only occur occasionally and default probabilities usually vary slowly over time, so pricing the potential for credit events to affect default probabilities need not require constant trading.

Theory predicts that when the information endowments of trading counterparties are heterogeneous, the party with the lesser information endowment will suffer greater costs of executing the trade. Generally, based on the reality of equity market trading, market microstructure theory has assumed that the market-maker is the uninformed trader and that his customers have information privileges. Hence, the wider observed bid-ask spreads, since the liquidity provider seeks to protect himself from his information disadvantage. As explained above, this relationship breaks down in bond markets.

Until recently, standard market microstructure models have been based on two different sets of traders: the informed and the uninformed. While uninformed traders only care about liquidating their positions, and therefore are less concerned with the timing of their trade, informed traders care more about immediacy, since the private information they hold concerning the value of an asset must be traded upon quickly. Their ability to advantageously observe the order flow represents an important source of private information for bond market dealers. The order flow in debt trading is indicative, as it can yield useful information to market-makers on how rival market-makers manage their inventories and on the fluctuations of market demand for particular securities. In other words, the privileged access of liquidity-providers to information they can infer from market-making activities (e.g. order flow that is 'internalised' and that they can exclusively view) gives them an edge over other dealers and, possibly, their less-valued clients.

iv.   Fundamentals of retail investor protection in bond markets

Asymmetric information

The protection of consumers has always been a priority for regulators in all markets, especially in cases where it is difficult for the buyer to properly ascertain the quality of the good or service that is purchased. Financial products and services require particularly diligent regulatory oversight to protect unsophisticated investors who not only are at an informational disadvantage from the start, but who are also susceptible to advice that can be biased from conflicts of interest *and* can only ascertain the quality of the product or service gradually over time. The incompleteness of financial contracts leads to a classic principal-agent problem, since the value of the service/product delivered depends largely on the diligence and honesty with which the agent executes the delegated task. In cases such as these, transaction costs are not limited to the cost of executing the transaction alone, but also comprise attendant costs related to: monitoring agent behaviour after the contract is signed, verifying product characteristics and whether disclosed information is accurate and complete, and reverting to the law in cases of fraud, breach of contract or failure to address conflicts of interest (Llewellyn, 1999).

When transaction costs are high, users may feel deterred from increasing their time opportunity cost of executing transactions by searching for best deals. This impatience, or the need for immediacy, makes the user more vulnerable to capture by his established broker/market-maker. Alternatively, high transaction costs can deter retail investors from even entering the market. This is especially true in times when public confidence in markets is low, as is the case today following a spate of financial scandals on both sides of the Atlantic. To the extent that mandating price transparency can reduce transaction costs and increase public confidence in markets, it will be a key instrument in the regulator's toolkit. Yet whether mandating a greater degree of price transparency will in fact drive down transaction costs remains a contentious debate, not least because – as a recent study by The Bond Market Association (2005a) shows – pre-trade transparency is already high in the EU sovereign debt market, and is rapidly coming to the fore in the corporate bond market.

A strategy for retail investor protection in bond markets

As a starting point, it is important to be mindful that no degree of legislation will guarantee full investor protection in any segment of the capital market. Fundamentally, investing in capital markets is a risky enterprise, because all investments are accompanied by an inherent, or systematic, component of risk that can never be fully diversified. Contrary to popular belief, principal invested in fixed income markets is therefore *always* at risk. No matter how secure an investment may seem, there is always a positive probability of default – however small – on one or more coupon payments and/or on the principal, as evidenced from the (admittedly rare) default on an investment grade issue. For example, since 1991, there have been four investment grade corporate debt defaults in the EU (S&P, 2005). The figures were significantly higher in the global debt market. Although there were no investment grade defaults in 2004, the last time this happened was in 1996. Since the year 2000, there were 28 investment grade defaults and 14 in the year 2002 alone (!) (S&P, 2005, Table 4.2).

Default need not mean loss of all, or even any, principal, since in the wake of a corporate bankruptcy, assets can be ring-fenced for certain classes of (senior) creditors. Nevertheless, defaults often do entail significant losses for investors, particularly of the retail variety, who tend to be lower down in the pecking order of bond investors during bankruptcy proceedings (particularly if their assets are not held in portfolios managed professionally).

Table 4.2 Corporate debt defaults in the EU

Year	Total defaults	Investment grade defaults	Speculative grade defaults	Default rate (%)	Investment grade default rate (%)	Speculative grade default rate (%)	Total debt defaulting (€ bil)
1991	1	0	1	0.76	0	50	
1992	0	0	0	0	0	0	
1993	1	0	1	0.51	0	20	
1994	0	0	0	0	0	0	
1995	0	0	0	0	0	0	
1996	0	0	0	0	0	0	
1997	0	0	0	0	0	0	
1998	0	0	0	0	0	0	
1999	5	0	5	0.86	0	6.58	0.74
2000	3	1	2	0.46	0.18	2.02	0.49
2001	8	0	8	1.09	0	7.27	2.21
2002	20	1	16	2.1	0.15	12.8	16.72
2003	8	2	5	0.82	0.28	3.4	11.72
2004	2	0	2	0.23	0	1.22	1.07

Source: Standard and Poor's.

In the debate on retail investor protection within the context of the upcoming Art. 65 review, perhaps too much attention has been paid to the issue of price transparency. Focusing only, or disproportionately, on the price transparency dimension is to reduce to a single issue what really is a multi-dimensional one. Retail investor protection in fixed income markets is best thought of as a vector of complementary components, which are listed in Table 4.3. To be fair, a number of these points have already been addressed in the new EU regulatory framework for securities markets, enshrined in the FSAP, which has extensively addressed conflicts of interest, information asymmetries between clients and service providers, etc. This table merely serves as a call for regulators to focus on what we believe to be the key elements of any regulatory strategy for investor protection in bond markets. In some cases, responding to the points below will only require proper implementation and enforcement of existing legislation rather than the creation of new legislation. In others, they may require new legislation, for example, if, subsequent to debate and cost-benefit analyses, it is decided that direct retail investor participation in the high-yield segment should be curtailed and it is mandated that their investments be channelled through funds

Table 4.3 Components of retail investor protection

Conflicts of interest	▪ Conflicts of interest in research and in the sales of wholesale type instruments to retail investors ought to be avoided through self-imposed or statutory measures, depending on the credibility of the former.
Education and information	▪ Policy measures should be taken to ensure that retail investors are aware of their rights and of the courses of action to which they are entitled when they perceive fraud. ▪ Raising awareness of associated risks is an essential component of enhancing investor protection. ▪ So is furthering investor's understanding of how liquidity is provided and behaves in the bond markets. ▪ Retail investors should be provided with information, including price information, that is clear and most relevant to their ability to make informed investment decisions. ▪ Principle of *caveat emptor* must be remembered.
Principal protection	▪ Far more important for retail investors than transaction cost reduction is to retain their principal, so policy measures ought to focus more on ways (not necessarily statutory rules) to minimise losses from default, rather than putting into place statutory rules that may save retail investors very little on transaction costs (since very few trades are executed per retail investor, unlike in equity markets) and damage market quality, especially liquidity, in the process.
Suitability of instruments	▪ Complex structured products, high-yield debt and other risky investments ought to be marketed to institutional and high-wealth, not average retail, investors. If the latter seek higher risk-return investments, they should be encouraged to go through funds.
Statutory regulation minimisation	▪ Statutory regulation minimisation is essential to preserving the competitiveness and dynamism of bond markets, so it is particularly important at the wholesale level. ▪ Nevertheless, it also yields benefits at the retail level. For example, aware of the risks they are undertaking, retail investors should be able to

	decide their own risk profiles. Clark (2005) discusses the need to protect retail investors from products that were specifically designed for the retail level, which can yield low returns, be subject to little competition, etc.
Fund use	▪ Retail investors ought to be encouraged to use funds, particularly for placements outside a select group of the highest quality (very low credit risk, high liquidity) corporate, government and quasi-government issues. ▪ There should not be mandatory channelling of retail investors through funds. Retail investors should have the option of direct participation in the bond market, at least for liquid, high-grade issues. This will provide an incentive to fund managers to offer competitive services to their clients, particularly in a fragmented market such as the EU, where competition between funds remains limited.
Transaction cost reduction	▪ Investors have the right to expect and should know how much they must pay in terms of transaction costs when trading bonds. In dealership markets, transaction fees related e.g. to trade clearing and settlement are subsumed into spreads, which also cover the cost of liquidity provision in terms of inventory risk, but retail investors should be able to discern whether they have been dealt a fair price, i.e. one that is competitive in the marketplace. ▪ Greater transparency in the determinants of bid-offer spreads would enhance competitive pressures among the broker-dealers. Price transparency is but one way among several to increase competition between market-makers or 'systematic internalisers'. ▪ Ultimately, technological progress creates the potential for transaction costs to fall. Nevertheless, it is important to remember that electronic trading need not necessarily reduce transaction costs, as this will rather depend on the business model adopted by its operator.
Documentation	▪ Event risk can strike suddenly, when investors (and even institutional investors and credit rating agencies) are caught unprepared. Thus,

	documentation plays a key role in protecting the principal of unsecured debt holders.
	▪ Measures to improve documentation, which ought to be market-led development, can nevertheless be encouraged by regulators.
Size of denominations	▪ Denomination sizes ought to be reduced, at least for the most liquid issues of creditworthy issuers, so as to allow retail investors to reap the benefits of direct investments in these issues. Doing so will also probably enhance the liquidity of these issues, as retail investors bring greater heterogeneity to the existing class of debt holders.

Educating investors

Unsophisticated investors may wrongly believe that their capital (principal invested) is safe and that they are guaranteed regular interest payments. Yet corporate bonds are by no means risk-free investments, as the rising number of fallen angels[100] suggests; high-yield corporate debt only yields attractive returns because the risk of default is anything but negligible. Likewise, the inverse relationship that prevails between interest rates and a bond's price is counterintuitive for those who (wrongly) believe that higher interest rates mean higher coupon payments on fixed rate bonds. This hypothesis was corroborated in a recent survey of US fixed income retail investors by the NASD: over 60% of retail investors were found to be unaware of interest rate risk.[101] That retail investors are becoming more active in bond markets is not a sufficient reason in and of itself to warrant regulatory intervention, as the industry has rightly pointed out on numerous occasions. Regulation cannot remove the probability of a company defaulting on its debt, nor can it remove interest rate risk. Parallel to due diligence requirements on the sell side, the buyer must also be judicious and apply common sense to any investment decision on the basis of *caveat emptor*. Investor education is therefore a primary pillar of investor protection.

---

[100] 'Fallen angels' is corporate jargon for formerly investment grade debt that was downgraded to junk status.

[101] See www.investinginbonds.com.

Conflicts of interest and suitability of instruments

Any regulation to improve bond investor protection should be preceded first and foremost by due diligence on the part of salespeople, in order to ensure that conflicts of interest are not guiding their advice to clients. Complex structured products, high-yield debt and other risky investments ought to be marketed to institutional and high-wealth, not average retail, investors, who know little about the fixed income business and have little capital to spare. This vector of investor protection has nothing to do with price transparency but is rather one of principles, or where principles are wanting, one of deterrence through fines and other penalties. Likewise, conflicts of interest in in-house research activities, where researchers take orders from colleagues in the front office or management to indirectly promote company products, can be a source of investor losses. Yet these can be (and have increasingly been) addressed by installing Chinese walls which serve to minimise opportunities for such conflicts of interest and the sale of wholesale-type instruments to retail investors ought to be avoided through self-imposed or statutory measures, depending on the credibility of the former.

Principal protection vs. transaction cost reduction

The central policy objective related to investor protection in bond markets ought not to be the elimination of risk (which is impossible), but to find ways for investors to minimise risk given their preferred risk profile. Because of the nature of fixed income (bond) investments and the risk that principal will not be recovered, principal protection ought to be the primary focus of regulatory efforts aimed at increasing the level of protection of retail investors. For the purpose of clarification, principal protection does not necessarily entail statutory rules that fundamentally alter the way business is conducted in fixed income markets. It may perhaps not even entail greater price transparency, although this assertion is quite debatable.[102] The point is rather that policy measures taken to reduce transaction costs for retail investors will not in any way guarantee

---

[102] Some regulators have argued, for example, that if retail investors had had easier and more immediate access to bond price information, they could have at least mitigated their losses in the numerous corporate defaults that have occurred in Europe in the past three years. Although the contrary view is that since this information would have been interpreted by the investors' advisors, what really matters is the quality of advice.

that their principal will be better protected. Thus, it is important for regulators to bear in mind that for the retail investor with capital placed in fixed income securities, the question of transaction costs is only trivial compared with the importance of preserving their principal. This is due to the fact that *although it is a component of investor protection, reducing transaction costs acquires far less importance in a setting of infrequent trading.* Despite this, investors have the right to expect and should know how much of the spread they pay is actually due to prevailing market conditions and what portion of it is actually covers transaction costs, because in dealership markets transaction fees such as clearing and settlement are all subsumed into spreads. Greater transparency in the determinants of bid-offer spreads would enhance competitive pressures among the broker-dealers.

If the ongoing electronisation of bond markets (although it is in the early stage, especially in the European corporate debt segment) eventually induces a shift in the nature of bond trading, so that assets that are relatively illiquid today trade hands more frequently in the future, then it will make sense for regulators to focus more on transaction costs faced by retail investors in bond markets. Most likely, the European corporate bond market especially has not reached that stage of maturity, so that in today's environment, principal protection ought to remain the focus.

Statutory regulation minimisation

Driven by technological progress, globalisation and the invention of new financial instruments, markets are evolving today at a rate that makes flexibility a top priority for all market actors. Regulators must take account of the degree and speed with which markets are evolving, and centre any regulatory strategy foremost on the amount of flexibility it offers market operators. In a world of such rapid change, regulations that seek to impose a top-down market architecture can deliver a fatal blow to the ability of markets to attract foreign capital. A world in which (constrained) regulatory competition is the norm necessitates careful attentiveness to the notion of efficient regulation which does not hinder market self-determination. In the words of Arthur Levitt, former Chairman of the SEC, the role of the regulator is not to

> ...impose or dictate the ultimate structure of markets [but] rather to establish, monitor and uphold [a regulatory] framework that gives competition the space and sustenance to flourish. Markets can then

develop according to "their own genius" for the ultimate benefit of investors.[103]

This position seems to be echoed by Charlie McCreevy, EU Commissioner for the Internal Market, who has outlined his programme for the next five years in a recent Green Paper on financial services,[104] which places great emphasis on market self-determination and competitiveness. Concerning the core of the current policy debate on liquidity versus transparency, as Wallenstein (2000) notes, it is important that regulatory efforts to improve liquidity remain sensitive to market structures, existing business models, and to the behavioural characteristics of the institutions participating in those markets. Otherwise, there is no guarantee that regulatory efforts will bear fruit and that liquidity would improve. In fact, liquidity could even recede. If this were the case, market quality would suffer, with adverse consequences for the welfare of retail investors.

Encourage use of funds

For many retail investors with little knowledge of fixed income markets and limited funds, one of the surest avenues of protection (relative to going it alone) may be to have recourse to professional investment advisors and to invest in funds, at least for sub-investment grade issues. First, due to the number of debt securities, it is very expensive for a single investor to hold a properly diversified portfolio, which is done efficiently through buying into a fund. In addition, unlike equity portfolios, bond portfolios generally have to hold many more securities in order to be diversified. This is due to the fact that equities can have significant upward, as well as downward, potential. Yet bond returns are characterised by an asymmetry between limited upward potential and absolute losses in case of a default.

There ought to be a serious policy debate in Europe about whether investments in fixed income securities by retail investors ought to be channelled into bond funds. Already, this is practiced in a few countries around the world, such as China. The basic idea is that investment professionals are better equipped to protect the capital of retail investors, not least because they have the ability to respond immediately to credit

---

[103] As quoted in Ruth (1999).

[104] See European Commission (2005).

developments, whereas even relatively sophisticated, financially literate retail investors usually respond to market developments with a long lag.

Nevertheless, *mandating* that funds act as the only channel of access to bond markets for retail investors is undesirable primarily for the reason that allowing direct participation in the market acts as a disciplining mechanism on funds. Without such an option, funds would not have the incentive to offer the best possible terms to their clients. Already, it is well-known that the fund industry in Europe is relatively inefficient compared to its American counterpart.

Perhaps the best way to proceed is to encourage/mandate retail investors to use bond funds for any investments below investment grade, or for fundamentally less liquid investment grade issues, while leaving the option open for them to have direct access to liquid, high-grade securities. An added advantage of the direct access option is that it can contribute to greater market liquidity, because retail investors represent a class that introduces greater heterogeneity into the market, with different characteristics, objectives and trading patterns than the wholesale players. As a result, liquidity improves.

Documentation

As the funding of European corporations continues to evolve from a model previously dominated by bank lending to a more market-oriented one, the locus of credit risk has diffused from a handful of credit institutions to manifold and dispersed investors. Nevertheless, legal and market structures have not evolved concomitantly with the shift to greater disintermediation in the European corporate debt market, so that banks retain disproportionate protection relative to bondholders (Eyerman & Hatton, 2004).

The disproportionate protection enjoyed by banks at the expense of the less concentrated remainder of an issue's bondholders results from the fact that in a crisis, fresh lending by banks, usually secured, automatically 'jumps the queue' in front of unsecured lenders. These latter may have been guaranteed in a bond covenant that secured lending would be capped at a certain amount, or a so-called 'negative pledge'. Part of the problem is that rating agencies usually do not take account of the weakness or strength of covenant packages in their assignment of ratings, so that bond investors may be completely unaware of the level of event risk they face.

In 2002, a group of 26 institutional investors, referred to collectively as the G-26 (Gang of 26), drafted a charter to strengthen bondholder rights in an attempt to call more attention to their demands for greater protection from event risk. Event risk can strike suddenly, when investors (and even institutional investors and credit rating agencies) are caught unprepared. Due to infighting and strategic positioning by the signers,[105] the G-26 charter never really went anywhere, but the precedent was important, as important lessons can be drawn from the exercise, first and foremost by bringing the issue of covenants and negative pledges more particularly to the fore. Nevertheless, this initiative has recently regained momentum with the involvement of the German asset management association, BVI. The question of negative pledges is one that ought not to be understated, especially since covenant protection is traditionally much weaker in continental Europe than it is in the British Isles (Hatton, 2005). Bolstering the effectiveness of negative pledges therefore constitutes one of the key avenues for enhancing the protection of bondholders' interests.[106]

4.4 Transparency and liquidity

One of the focal points of the ongoing policy debate concerns liquidity – and how it can be enhanced by various regulations (e.g. on price transparency), since liquidity is probably the best metric by which to measure market quality.

i. What is liquidity and how to define it?

What is liquidity and what are its properties/benefits that make it so desirable a policy objective for financial markets? As noted by Frank Fernandez (1999), liquidity is the lifeblood of financial markets. There is hardly an area of financial activity that is not explicitly or implicitly tied to liquidity. It affects asset pricing, credit risk, financial market development, capital structure, option pricing, market microstructure, and monetary

---

[105] In order to be truly effective, the G-26 proposal would have had to have been adopted by a wider group of investors and they must have agreed in concert to refuse to buy debt from issuers that do not ensure the effectiveness of negative pledges. Evidently, game theory predicts that such a situation is unsustainable. One or several investors would be too tempted to buy up attractive issues, even if the collective demands of the G-26 had not been met.

[106] A negative pledge is a clause in a bond covenant that provides some protection for unsecured borrowers against event risk.

policy.[107] Liquid debt securities provide tangible benefits to investors, issuers and other active participants in capital markets, such as central banks.[108] Secondary market liquidity is an important factor in determining portfolio choice; in reducing credit risk and promoting financial stability; in determining capital structure; in reducing transactions costs from trading activities; and in reducing flotation costs.

Various definitions of liquidity exist, without there being a consensus on what exactly is meant by liquidity. Table 4.4 gives an overview of all the variables that are commonly used to proxy liquidity. Measuring liquidity effects is not an easy task, especially as the interaction between liquidity and expected returns may be non-linear (Amihud & Mendelson, 1986).

Table 4.4 Measuring corporate bond liquidity: Individual securities

	Theoretical relation to liquidity	Empirical relation to liquidity
Issued amount	*Predicts a positive correlation*: Larger issues should trade more often because: 1) More investors hold the security, decreasing costs of information and increasing trading volume for portfolio optimisation 2) Market-makers more willing to transact: inventory holding costs are lower because lower information costs due to more coverage/analysis/recognition and higher trading volume	Less robust than theoretical predictions: *both positive and negative correlations* have been identified: some large issues relatively illiquid and some small issues relatively liquid
Age (time from issuance)	*Predicts a negative correlation*: The closer an issue is to maturity, the less liquid it becomes: 1) Lead manager commitment to making market in the newly issued bond only a short-term obligation 2) New issues tend to be under-priced so speculative trading is rife immediately after issue	Theoretical predictions are verified and even strongly confirmed in empirical results: *strong negative correlation,* as shown by yields rising with age (increasing transaction costs)

---

[107] See O'Hara (2004).

[108] Central banks hold liquid debt securities as reserve assets because large amounts can be bought or sold with little impact on the price (Fleming, 2001). Effectively, a liquid portfolio for a central bank amounts to a very low risk of incurring major capital losses while conducting open market operations.

	3) Issue is absorbed into buy-and-hold portfolios, so trading tends to decline with time	
Price volatility	*Predicts a negative correlation*: the higher the volatility of a security's price, the more illiquid it becomes: price volatility means greater unpredictability of price movements and more risk undertaken by the market-maker, so spreads widen, increasing cost of trading	*Mixed picture*: mostly a positive correlation: bid-ask spreads widen as volatility increases; but some studies show trading volume increases with price volatility, thus pushing down the liquidity premium
Yield dispersion	*Predicts a negative correlation*: if yield dispersion widens, market participants are less in agreement on value of a bond, increasing uncertainty and driving up liquidity premium	*No empirical evidence*
Missing prices	*Predicts a positive correlation*: A good indicator of the illiquidity of a bond is the reported end-of-the-day price if intra-day data are not available. If the price at the end of the day is identical to that of the previous day, it is highly likely the bond did not trade; likewise if there is a missing price.	*Little empirical evidence*
Spreads	*Predicts a negative correlation*: 1) If spreads widen, incentives to trade fall as transaction costs rise 2) Causality may run the other way also because wider spreads may simply reflect that the bond in question is illiquid for structural, as opposed to market structure, reasons	Many studies show unambiguous *negative correlation* between spreads and liquidity, with widening spreads being both a cause and a consequence of greater illiquidity
Market participants	*Predicts a positive correlation*: The greater the number of active traders, the greater the probability that at any given point, dealers will want to re-balance their inventories and investors their portfolios	Generally a *positive correlation*, although studies for bond markets have been very limited

Source: Authors, with cell content largely based on literature review by Houweling et al. (2003, pp. 9-14).

ii.   How liquidity affects asset pricing

There is an important link between liquidity and proper asset valuation. Asset pricing depends to a certain extent on liquidity. Recent evidence suggests that liquidity risk in bond markets is priced (de Jong & Driessen, 2004; Amihud & Mendelson, 1991; Elton & Green, 1998). Thus, liquidity has very real *economic* effects. By affecting asset pricing, liquidity affects the allocation of capital in both a static and a dynamic context.

Typically, an asset's *equilibrium* value is determined on the basis of the present discounted value of future cash flows and their risk, whether relative to the portfolio held by an investor or relative to the probability it will yield the expected cash flows. The yield spreads of corporate bonds over (virtually) risk-free government debt are far too large to be explained by historical default rates alone. This conundrum is even more pronounced in the high rated segment of the market, where default probabilities are very low, but where variations in credit spreads persist and remain inexplicably large in absolute terms (De Jong & Driessen, 2004). According to many researchers, the abnormally wide spread of corporate bond yields over risk-free assets compared with that justified by historical default patterns is best explained as the pricing of liquidity risk. The so-called 'liquidity premium' can be thought of as the equivalent of buying an option contract, since liquidity allows an investor to move swiftly into and out of positions with little risk of exposing himself to adverse price movements.

iii.   Liquidity and financial market efficiency

Efficient capital markets are characterised by the quick exploitation of arbitrage opportunities. Arbitrage can have a static as well as a dynamic dimension. In static terms, it means that cross-sectional discrepancies in pricing, say between inter-linked asset markets such as futures and the underlying cash market, disappear almost instantaneously. In a dynamic setting, liquidity contributes to the informational efficiency of markets. Information efficiency is often measured as the speed of convergence of a security's price upon its fundamental value. The more liquid an asset, other things such as information endowments being equal, the more likely it will converge rapidly upon its true economic value. The dynamics of price discovery are therefore facilitated by liquidity, which feeds back into greater pricing efficiency. Efficient price formation means that observable prices integrate *all* available information related to an asset's price, which ultimately leads to efficient resource/risk allocation. Thus, liquidity contributes materially to the fundamental purpose of financial markets, which is to allocate capital (and risk) efficiently on the basis of observed or expected prices.[109]

Another way to emphasis the importance of liquidity is by reviewing how market efficiency suffers from illiquidity. Liquidity suffers from high transaction costs to trading. For example, when market-makers enjoy a quasi-monopoly, they can charge wider bid-ask spreads in inter-dealer and dealer-to-customer trades, reducing the incentives for counterparties to trade and thereby reducing trading volume. Likewise, liquidity can suffer from various impediments to trading such as poor market design (structural illiquidity), imperfections in the trading infrastructure (leading to trading frictions), increasing market fragmentation, and illogical behavioural patterns by market participants, related to trader/investor/market-maker sentiment, such that e.g. asset prices over- and under-shoot their fundamental values, or e.g. market liquidity can suddenly and inexplicably dry up, particularly in times of market stress, as in the case of 'liquidity black holes'.[110] Very evidently, illiquidity hurts price discovery, as shown by Furfine & Remolona (2002), since the price impact of trades increases in times of market stress [illiquidity] (Fleming, 2001).

In sum, liquidity is essential for:
- the price discovery process
- asset pricing
- the rate and quality of assimilation of new information into asset prices
- capital structure decisions
- portfolio strategy decisions
- risk-taking and hedging
- flexibility (equivalent to an 'option' for traders to buy or sell)
- developing market structure.

---

[109] Arbitrage here is considered a behaviour that is beneficial to market efficiency, since it relates to mean-reverting speculation that drives assets back to their fundamental values. That is, price formation is a stable system. Yet there also exist forms of destabilising speculation that drive prices away from a stable equilibrium. Arbitrage, interpreted as the deliberate riding on the directional momentum of trading in order to make short-term profits, can lead to market imbalances, and ultimately, to a financial crisis. If liquidity is used by traders to engage in destabilising speculation, one wonders whether it is so desirable after all.

[110] See Persaud (2000).

The importance of liquidity in ensuring the economic efficiency of capital markets means that the role of public policy is vital: if misdirected, public policy can seriously harm the liquidity .of markets; on the other hand, regulations that foster higher-quality markets at little cost are beneficial to the economy.

iv.   Transparency

Does transparency in bond markets increase liquidity? The market microstructure literature has established that while a certain degree of transparency is good for overall market efficiency and liquidity, there is a point at which transparency may conflict with liquidity provision. In other words, as the degree of transparency increases, welfare gains initially rise, but subsequently fall as too demanding requirements could lead dealers to withdraw from market-making. This realisation leads one to raise the question: what degree of transparency is desirable? Can one talk of an optimal degree of transparency? If such a concept exists, how to reach it?

Unfortunately, very little research, whether theoretical or empirical, exists on bond market microstructure, so it is difficult, if not impossible, to answer these questions today. Wallenstein (2000) calls the corporate bond market one of the most empirically understudied areas of the economy. Two reasons can explain the absence of extensive research on bond market microstructure: first, the inter-dealer market, by far the largest component, is known to be very opaque to non-market participants, because of its sheer size and diversity. The lack of publicly available statistics and more general information about the organisation of these markets has stifled attempts by researchers to identify with any degree of precision what, if any, inefficiencies and market failures may arise and whether regulators' calls for more transparency are justified or not. A second reason is that as a self-regulated, inter-dealer market that is widely perceived to be running smoothly, the OTC bond market has attracted less attention due to the limited scope for public policy intervention. The lack of centralised reporting of trades,[111] resulting from the very small share of transactions that are exchange-traded as opposed to being conducted over-the-counter, is seen to be one of the main culprits.[112] However, the question must be

---

[111] This situation has since change in the United States with the introduction of the TRACE system.

[112] See Wallenstein (2000, p. 124).

asked why these markets have developed as OTC and what the (potentially harmful) consequence would be of a 'concentration rule' for bonds. That there does not exist any significant literature on the subject, as related to bond markets, complicates the task of analysis. We will therefore limit ourselves to raising a few questions and to reviewing the US experience with TRACE and drawing lessons from it for the EU.

What may appear to be a clear mandate for policy to improve liquidity will be misguided if the relation is the inverse of the one described above. In other words, transaction costs may be higher precisely because certain securities fundamentally lack liquidity. This brings us to the cause of the lack of liquidity. Is the dearth of liquidity due to the patterns of investment by the holders of debt securities, or the wide variety of bonds that preclude the exposure of investors' capital to more than a few (in terms of direct investments, that is, as opposed to funds)? There is some evidence for this. Or is trading in some securities thin because they are illiquid and therefore imply a higher transaction cost that could negate the trading profits that could accrue? While in some markets it appears that market liquidity can be improved by mandating that market-makers adopt certain provisions, such as price transparency, such provisions will do little or nothing to improve the liquidity of a fundamentally illiquid asset, or one that quickly becomes illiquid (such as most corporate bonds after their first few days or weeks of issuance). In a case such as this, introducing price transparency will only create costs for the market-maker, with few benefits in the form of enhanced liquidity. For example, as Edwards et al. (2004) report, of the 70,000 TRACE-eligible securities, only 22,453 traded more than once in the whole of 2003 (!). As a final point, it is important that regulators be mindful that increased price transparency will not eradicate fraudulent practices by bond issuers, or misleading information or conduct by underwriters, especially practices that could put an investor's principal at risk.

v.   Degree of price transparency in US and EU bond markets

A recent study published by The Bond Market Association (2005a) on the current state of price transparency in European bond markets finds that both pre- and post-trade price disclosure is high in the EU, at least for wholesale players in government debt securities. Corporate bond price transparency, meanwhile, has been improving steadily, according to the same report.

While the obligation to publish trades no later than 15 minutes after trade execution in the US market gives a powerful impetus to extending price transparency to retail trades, unsophisticated bond investors in the EU currently do not enjoy such a privilege, at least not directly (they could obtain the information indirectly through their broker or data vendors). What is more, by July 2005, the time threshold for post-trade price dissemination in the US had been cut twice since the introduction of TRACE (see Box 4.1) – a post-trade reporting service that became operational in July 2002 – and is now set at 15 minutes.

Box 4.1 The US TRACE system

Transaction information that traders are obliged to report to NASD:

- NASD symbol
- Number of bonds traded
- Price (and state commission)
- Indication of whether the trade was a buy, sell or cross
- Date of trade execution
- Counterparty identifier
- Principal, agent or agency cross
- Time of trade execution
- Reporting side executing broker in case of 'give up trade'
- Counterparty introducing broker in case of 'give up trade'
- Stated commission
- Trade modifiers
- Yield

Dissemination of reported information would follow these conventions:

- Must be TRACE eligible security (i.e., only SEC-registered US and foreign firms, investment and non-investment grade, and dollar denominated debt that is depository eligible)
- Security whose initial issuance size was over $1 billion, whether investment grade or not
- If reported trade size > $5 million, an identifier for large trades will replace the exact amount traded with the symbol 5MM+ (old pre-TRACE FIPS rules had set the floor at $1 million)
- Timeframe for price dissemination after a trade initially set at 75 minutes, and subsequently was reduced to 15 minutes.

Source: Put together from Ayanian (2002).

A good starting point for analysing the potential impact of any future EU regulation of bond markets is to first look in detail at the US experience with price transparency in the corporate debt market and draw the lessons that can be learned from that experience. The introduction of TRACE, and, to a lesser extent, its precursor FIPS, and the wealth of data it generates for researchers has led to greater interest in econometric studies on bond markets.

Nevertheless, the few studies that do exist tend to focus on the American municipal bond market, whose particularities render the transposition of these studies' conclusions to the international bond market or to European bond markets somewhat risky. TRACE, and its creation was motivated by the realisation that post-trade transparency plays an important role in bond market price discovery and that price dissemination allows all market participants to obtain a better insight into the quality of the prices offered (since in a dynamic context and in liquid markets, post-trade transparency contributes to pre-trade transparency). Perhaps more importantly, price dissemination can contribute in a material way to the creation of a single investor 'market price' for any given (liquid) security. Finally the greater inter-connectedness of trading platforms gave investors more choice and stiffened competition between market-makers.

Interestingly, some academic studies in the US have taken data from the TRACE system to analyse whether investor savings were at all significant after the introduction of the dissemination system. Perhaps the most cited among these is the paper by Edwards & Piwowar (2004), who claim that TRACE has realised tremendous gains for retail investors by reducing transaction costs very substantially (on the order of $2 billion, and these authors even argue that their chosen econometric methodology has understated the total savings). Controversy surrounding their chosen method of analysis continues to swirl, however, not least because it remains uncertain whether the reduced transaction costs were merely correlated with, as opposed to driven by, increased price transparency. For example, market participants claim to have observed similar reductions in transaction costs in bond markets in Europe over the same time period as a result of lower volatility (mirrored in the US market), enhanced market-driven pre-trade transparency and greater competition among dealers for order flow.

No academic or other study that we are aware of has made a systematic assessment of corporate bond transaction costs in the EU. Undoubtedly, the absence of widespread data dissemination is an important factor in that research void. Data reported in the TRAX system, published by its operator, the ICMA, remains less detailed than the TRACE system, and it is impossible to track any degree of information from the transaction costs of individual trades. In practice, the same criticism can be made of the TRACE data, since the spreads prevailing at the time of a trade are not published). With the current limited availability of detailed data in the EU, it is difficult for market analysts and researchers alike to ascertain the true level of liquidity in bond markets. Although traders and other professionals active in the markets will have a better idea than academics, regulators and central bankers perhaps of the level of liquidity prevailing at a point in time, the scenario of fragmented markets without a central reporting system where trade quotes can be obtained for trading purposes probably makes it difficult for smaller players to obtain a completely accurate picture of overall market liquidity. Such a scenario has the potential to generate adverse welfare consequences by benefiting large market dealers at the expense of smaller ones.

While it may still be too early to tell, there are indications that the implementation has been beneficial. Industry executives and regulators share an overall positive opinion of TRACE. One must consider how ambitious the project was, given the context in which it was introduced. A largely opaque secondary market in corporate bonds was converted through a process of phased implementation and subject to careful regulatory and industry oversight, into a largely transparent one, although certain concerns have been expressed regarding the impact of TRACE on liquidity in lower-rated securities.

Regulatory concerns surrounding bond markets are complicated by the fact that they are overwhelmingly an institutional, as opposed to retail, market. Even within the category of institutions, the great majority of bond trading is conducted in the inter-dealer market, not dealer-to-customer, where the customer is an institutional investor along the lines of a mutual or pension fund. But the fact that direct retail participation in the market is non-existent or minimal and that institutional investors have the sophistication to master the ins and outs of the bond market is not in itself an argument against price transparency. If institutional investors, such as mutual funds, face high transaction costs from trading in bond markets, there are direct costs to the retail investor, albeit the costs are accrued indirectly, first through the intermediary of the investment firm. It is unlikely that a fund would not pass on the costs of trading at excessive spreads to the customer, lowering the latter's return on investment. Nevertheless, if institutional investors as a group feel that price transparency ought to be improved, there is every reason to expect that, as faithful clients of market-makers, their request would be honoured by at least some liquidity providers. After all, such an outcome is only natural in competitive markets. As the TBMA report (2005a) records, that is exactly what appears to have happened in Europe since 2002.

As a final point, in the current policy debate on the MiFID application to bonds, the question of transparency is often limited to the dimension of price transparency for trade reporting purposes. But in the regulator's eyes, transparency as a policy objective goes deeper than mere post-trade transparency and is guided by the philosophy that market activity ought not to be taking place behind a veil. There are four policy objectives that fall under the umbrella of transparency, which is seen as necessary to maintain: 1) financial stability, 2) retail investor protection, 3) competition among financial services providers and 4) capital markets that discourage fraudulent and criminal activity. The benefits of market transparency do not derive from price transparency alone, which is but one component of it.

The most pressing challenge ahead for EU regulators revolves around designing a regulatory framework that simultaneously encourages and facilitates further retail participation in bond markets without impacting on the competitiveness of EU financial markets and on the principle of market self-determination. An important final point is also that retail investor protection in bond markets is not necessarily ensured by even full price transparency, since those conditions do not in any way guarantee that the investor will recuperate the entirety of his invested principal. As mentioned above, the most important objective related to retail investor protection ought not to be transaction costs (albeit still important as a secondary objective), but rather the safeguarding of principal, which is fundamentally a credit (and therefore corporate governance and accounting issue).

Ultimately, whether transparency ought to be increased in fixed income markets by regulatory measures depends very much on the ultimate goal of such a policy measure. If the objective is enhanced retail investor protection, this policy may well be misguided, since the key to the protection of retail investors in fixed income markets, unlike in equities, is the preservation of principal, because retail investors invest in fixed income precisely because they feel they can get a steady cash flow from coupon payments without any risk of losing their capital. On the other hand, if increased price transparency is considered in order to enhance market liquidity, this policy measure requires careful consideration. The academic literature is not helpful. In other words, it is too early to discern the nature of the relationship between liquidity and price transparency.

5. Conclusions

There are preliminary indications today that the European Commission might seek to enhance transparency in the bond market under the dual argument of increasing investor protection and improving market efficiency. For a number of reasons elucidated in this report, we urge measured and deliberate action on the part of regulators as they embark on the MiFID Art. 65 review, because it is by no means clear that transparency is the best policy instrument to address either of these concerns. This caveat is motivated by the following concerns:

- **The unclear nature of the relationship between price transparency and liquidity**

The exact nature of the relationship between price transparency and liquidity remains a contentious matter and most of the academic research has pointed to a non-linear association between the two variables. That is, liquidity is initially found to improve as transparency increases, but too much transparency can damage liquidity. Too much transparency has the potential to damage the liquidity-providing function by discouraging market-makers from risking their capital to supply it, which would reduce market efficiency. There is certainly not enough evidence on an unambiguous or linear relationship between price transparency and liquidity at this point that would warrant statutory measures aimed at improving price transparency in the European bond market in the name of market efficiency. Thus, blanket transparency requirements covering the entire universe of bonds are likely to hurt liquidity and reduce market efficiency in some market segments, particularly in already less liquid instruments. As far as retail investor protection is concerned, one can question to what extent transparency is the right policy instrument to meet this objective.

- **The likelihood that greater transparency is not a win-win situation for all market participants: some are likely to be worse off**

It is not clear that increasing transparency would lead to a win-win situation for all market participants. In fact, there is evidence to the contrary. For example, when MTS introduced anonymity of trading on its Italian platform in 1997, liquidity improved and transaction costs fell for institutional investors who traded in large blocks. Nevertheless, there are also both theoretical and empirical examples indicating that increasing transparency increases the costs of liquidity provision and the costs for investors to unwind large positions. For example, the introduction of the TRACE post-trade reporting system in the US has lowered transaction costs for retail investors making direct investments. However, it may have increased transaction costs for institutional investors. Since the vast majority of retail investments in fixed income are channelled through funds, such policy measures designed by regulators to protect retail investors might paradoxically damage the very interests they are designed to protect, as funds pass on higher transaction costs to their retail clients, e.g. in the form of lower returns.

- **The risk that excessive attention is placed on transaction costs, rather than principal protection, in a regulatory strategy for retail investor protection**

Bid-ask spreads, or transaction costs more generally, ought not to be considered the only criterion for judging market quality. If the primary objective of introducing greater price transparency into bond markets is to reduce bid-ask spreads, market quality does not necessarily improve as a result, and transaction costs need not necessarily fall either. In addition, in the case of bond market segments characterised by infrequent trading, reducing transaction costs is a secondary concern compared with minimising the risks of not recovering the principal.

If the objective guiding a regulatory strategy to improve transparency is to enhance retail investor protection, focusing on transaction costs may well be misguided policy: the key to the protection of retail investors in fixed income markets, unlike in equities, is the preservation of principal, rather than minimising transaction costs. True, transaction costs for the retail investor will probably fall if the Commission were to mandate greater post-trade transparency. Nevertheless, the typical retail investor follows a buy-and-hold strategy in fixed income investments. Within such a strategy, only twice in the lifetime of the investment are transaction costs incurred: when the asset is purchased and when it is sold at maturity.

Retail bond trades are infrequent, and retail investors invest in fixed income assets precisely because they often mistakenly feel they can get a steady cash flow from coupon payments without incurring any risk of losing their capital. Therefore, the focus of policy-makers in the field of investor protection ought to be on the points elicited in our strategy for retail transactions in debt securities: investor education, suitability of instruments, principal protection, reducing conflicts of interest, encouraging fund use, and, as an objective secondary to these, ultimately, transaction cost reduction.

- **Related to the preceding point, a danger that what is essentially a wholesale market is fundamentally redesigned to suit the needs of the minute group of retail investors who seek direct access**

Bond markets remain an overwhelmingly wholesale business in terms of traded volumes. Whatever retail participation there is, it is usually indirect. One must therefore question to what extent investor protection concerns ought to be the primordial regulatory imperative—as opposed to market liquidity or efficiency, for example—and whether the policy debate is excessively influenced by these concerns. Policy decisions may entail trade-offs between regulatory objectives. In the face of such a trade-off, it is not clear why investor protection concerns—when they are addressed by measures that may be inimical to market liquidity, such as e.g. greater price transparency—ought to be the overriding imperative given the wholesale nature of the bond business.

Therefore, there ought to be a serious policy debate on whether direct retail participation in bond markets, for sub-investment grade securities and less liquid investment grade issues should be curtailed in order to prevent retail investor concerns from driving the design of markets when the retail segment of the market is so small compared to the inter-dealer and institutional segments.

At the same time, we do not recommend the *mandatory* use of funds for retail investors across all debt classes, particularly in very liquid EU or US government bonds or liquid, highly-rated corporate debt securities. Direct retail investor participation in bond markets enhances market liquidity and acts as a disciplining mechanism on bond funds. This consideration is all the more important in an environment such as the EU, where asset management is known to be far below its potential efficiency and where competitive forces are not yet given a free rein.

The central policy objective related to investor protection in bond markets ought therefore not to be the elimination of risk (which is impossible) but to find ways for investors to minimise risk, given their preferred risk profile.

- **The different transparency imperatives for equity markets and bond markets, and even in various segments of the bond universe**

If the Commission were to mandate provisions for pre- and post-trade transparency in bond markets, it should not create blanket provisions that cover the whole fixed income universe, as is the case for equities. This is due to the recognition that typically, one equity share exists for a firm, whereas the same firm can issue hundreds of bonds in different currencies and with different maturities, risk profiles and yields, options such as convertibility into equity shares, seniority, etc. As a result, if regulators pursue transparency, statutory transparency requirements should be carefully tailored to specific market segments. For example, there is little economic justification for imposing costs on market-makers to increase post-trade transparency of fundamentally illiquid bonds that trade less than once a year. The value at which the last trade was conducted may be of no economic significance whatsoever a year later. The vast majority of corporate bonds hardly ever trade hands: for example, of the 70,000 or so TRACE-eligible corporate bonds, only some 22,000 were traded in 2003.

Occasionally, market regulation is influenced by lessons learned from academic research. For a variety of reasons, research on market microstructure has focused almost exclusively on equities. Virtually no academic literature exists on bond market microstructure. As a result, regulators must be careful not to draw hasty conclusions from such equity-centric literature. As we have shown in Chapter 4, the numerous differences between stocks and bonds, not only in their characteristics, but also in their investor base, holding patterns and surrounding market architectures, render the applicability of theoretical models developed in the academic literature to bond markets questionable at best.

- **The risk that regulation imposes a top-down market architecture that reduces flexibility and innovation**

Before the Commission mandates greater price transparency in bond markets, it ought to assess to what extent market-driven solutions can deliver the same result in a more efficient and market-friendly (and hence growth-friendly) way. For example, technological progress and financial innovation have led to a marked improvement in pre-trade transparency in the European bond market, in the form of inter-connected electronic trading platforms.

A central facet of any regulatory strategy is to clearly identify market failures and, conditional on this, to find the appropriate and least costly regulatory instrument to address a specific market failure. Whether transparency ought to be increased in fixed income markets depends very much on the ultimate goal of such a policy measure. As we explained in the report and above, whether transparency is the best instrument to pursue the objectives of investor protection and a smooth operation of securities markets in the bond universe is highly debatable.

Above all, the very successful evolution of (corporate) bond markets within an almost exclusively self-regulatory framework over the past few decades, coupled with their explosive rates of growth and innovation, imposes a certain responsibility on the part of regulators to proceed slowly and with great caution, if and when they deem it necessary to intervene with new statutory measures. These conclusions are all the more important in the context of the Lisbon Agenda, as the EU struggles to restore growth and competitiveness to flagging national economies.

- **The danger of seeing transparency as an end in itself without properly assessing whether it is economically justified**

It is not clear why bond market transparency should be an end in and of itself, and there is no economic justification for treating market transparency as an end for regulators to pursue for its own sake. As it stands, the MiFID does not sufficiently spell out why more, rather than less, transparency is desirable. For example, the recitals of MiFID only argue that transparency is necessary to achieve the regulatory objectives of "protecting investors and ensuring the smooth operation of securities markets". These recitals do not explain what are the mechanisms by which transparency leads to enhanced market efficiency and investor protection, nor do they recognise the possibility of a trade-off between transparency and liquidity. In other words, greater transparency could precisely lead to a less smooth functioning of securities markets, and hence may not be the proper instrument (at least in certain market segments) to pursue the objective of market efficiency or stability.

BIBLIOGRAPHY

Allen, H., J. Hawkins and S. Sato (2001), "Electronic trading and its implications for financial systems", *Electronic Finance: A New Perspective and Challenges*, BIS Papers No. 7, Bank for International Settlements, Basel.

Amihud, Yakov and Haim Mendelson (1986), "Asset Pricing and the Bid-Ask Spread", *Journal of Financial Economics*, Vol. 17, pp. 223-249.

———— (1991), "Liquidity, Maturity, and the Yields on US Treasury Securities", *Journal of Finance*, Vol. 46, pp. 1411-1425.

Andersen, Jens Verner and Per Plougmand Baertelsen (2004), "Liquidity and Transparency in the Danish Government Bond Market", *Monetary Review*, Danmarks Nationalbank, 2nd Quarter.

Ayanian, John (2002), "Corporate Bond Market Transparency and Debt Mark-Up Regulation", paper presented at the Bond Market Association Regional Bond Dealers Management Conference, Orlando, Florida, 30 January–1 February.

Baele, Lieven, Annalisa Ferrando, Peter Hördahl, Elizaveta Krylova and Cyril Monnet (2004), *Measuring Financial Integration in the Euro Area*, ECB Occasional Paper No. 14, European Central Bank, Frankfurt, May.

Bank for International Settlements (BIS) (2003), *Guide to the International Financial Statistics*, BIS Papers No. 14, February, pp. 13-14.

———— (2004), http://www.bis.org/publ/rpfx05a.pdf.

———— (2005), "Financial Markets Integration in Europe: The ECB's View", speech by Jean-Claude Trichet, *BIS Review*, 39/2005.

Bartram, Söhnke and Frank Fehle (2004), "Competition among Alternative Option Market Structures: Evidence from Eurex vs. Euwax", unpublished paper.

Batten, Jonathan, Thomas Fetherston and Peter Szilagyi (eds) (2004), *European Fixed Income Markets: Money, Bond, and Interest Rate Derivatives*, New Jersey: John Wiley & Sons, Ltd.

Bearing Point (2005), *The Electronic Bond Market 2005: An Analysis of the Electronic Bond Market in the Eurozone*.

Beck, Thorsten, Ross Levine and Norman Loayza (1999), *Financial Intermediation and Growth: Causality and Causes*, Central Bank of Chile Working Paper 56, Santiago.

Bessembinder, Hendrik, William Maxwell and Kumar Venkataraman (2005), "Optimal Market Transparency: Evidence from the Initiation of Trade Reporting in Corporate Bonds", unpublished paper.

Blommenstein, Hans (1998), "The Role of Banks in Capital Markets: Structural Changes, Functioning and Prospects for the 21st Century", in Shahid Javed Burki and Guillermo E. Perry (eds), *Banks and Capital Markets: Sound Financial Systems for the 21st Century*, Annual World Bank Conference on Development in Latin America and the Caribbean, San Salvador, El Salvador.

Bradberry, Adam (2005), "UK Regulator Plans to Fine Citigroup over Bond Trade", *Wall Street Journal*, 30 May.

Camdessus, Michel (1999), "Stable and Efficient Financial Systems for the 21st Century: A Quest for Transparency and Standards", paper presented at the 24th Annual IOSCO Conference, Lisbon.

Chae, Joon and Albert Wang (2004), "Who Makes Markets? The Role of Dealers and Liquidity Provision", unpublished paper, Massachusetts Institute of Technology, Cambridge, MA.

Chemmanur, T. and P. Fulghieri (1994), "Investment Bank Reputation, Information Production, and Financial Intermediation", *Journal of Finance*, Vol. 54, pp. 57-76.

Cheung, Chung, Frank de Jong and Barbara Rindi (2005), *Trading European Sovereign Bonds: The Microstructure of the MTS Trading Platform*, ECB Working Paper Series No. 432, European Central Bank, Frankfurt.

Chordia, Tarun, Richard Roll and Avanidhar Subrahmanyam (2000), "Commonality in Liquidity", *Journal of Financial Economics*, Vol. 56, pp. 3-28.

Christie, W. and P. Schultz (1994), "Why do NASDAQ Market-makers Avoid Odd-Eighth Quotes?", *Journal of Finance*, Vol. 49, pp. 1813-1840.

Chung, Joanna (2005), "Fitch turns negative on Italy and Portugal", *Financial Times*, 29 June.

Clark, David O. (2005), "Liquidity and transparency in the bond markets: Is there a trade off?", personal view, presentation to the Centre for

European Policy Studies workshop on European Bond Markets: Quo vadis, Regulator?, Brussels, 17 May.

Davis, Philip E. (2001), *Multiple Avenues of Intermediation, Corporate Finance and Financial Stability*, IMF Working Paper, 01/115, International Monetary Fund, Washington, D.C.

───── (2002), "Institutional Investors, Corporate Governance and the Performance of the Corporate Sector", *Economic Systems*, Vol. 26, Issue 3, pp. 203-229.

De Bondt, Gabe (2002), *Euro Area Corporate Debt Securities Market*, ECB Working Paper No. 164, European Central Bank, Frankfurt.

De Bondt, G. and D. Marqués-Ibáñez (2005), "High-yield bond diffusion in the United States, the United Kingdom and the euro area", *Journal of Financial Services Research*, Vol. 27 (2), pp. 163-181.

de Jong, Frank and Joost Driessen (2004), "Liquidity Premia in Corporate Bond and Equity Markets", University of Amsterdam, unpublished paper.

Dutordoir, Marie and Linda Van de Gucht (2004), "Determinants of Stockholder Reactions to Convertible Debt, Offering Announcements: An Analysis of the Western European Market", paper prepared for the Meetings of the EFMA (European Financial Management Association), Basel, 30 June–3 July.

ECB (2004), *The Euro Bond Market Study*, December.

───── (2005a), *Government Debt Management in the Euro Area - Recent Theoretical Developments and Changes in Practices*, Occasional Paper No. 25, Frankfurt, March.

───── (2005b), *Trading European Sovereign Bonds: The Microstructure of the MTS Trading Platform*, ECB Working Paper Series No. 432, Frankfurt.

[The] Economist (2005), "The Market and Methuselah", 10 February.

Edison, Hali, Ross Levine, Luca A. Ricci and Torsten M. Slok (2002), *International Financial Integration and Economic Growth*, IMF Working Paper 02/145, International Monetary Fund, Washington, D.C.

Edwards, A., L. Harris and M. Piwowar (2004), *Corporate Bond Market Transparency and Transaction Costs*, US SEC Working Document, Securities and Exchange Commission, Washington, D.C.

Eijffinger, Sylvester and E. Schaling (1993), "Central Bank Independence in Twelve Industrial Countries", *Quarterly Review*, Banca Nazionale del Lavoro, Vol. 184, pp. 49-89.

Ellis, Katrina, Roni Michaely and Maureen O'Hara (2005), "Competition in Investment Banking: Proactive, Reactive, or Retaliatory?", Cornell University, unpublished paper.

Elton, E.J. and T.C. Green (1998), "Tax and Liquidity Effects in Pricing Government Bonds", *Journal of Finance*, Vol. 53, No. 5, pp. 1533-1562.

Esho, Neil, Michael Kollo and Ian Sharpe (2004), *Eurobond Underwriter Spreads*, Financial Markets Group Discussion Paper 503, London School of Economics.

European Commission (2002), *The EU Economy: 2002 Review*, Brussels.

───── (2004), *Green Paper on Confronting Demographic Change: A New Solidarity between the Generations*, Brussels, 16.3.2005. COM(2005) 94 final.

───── (2005), *Green Paper on Financial Services*, 2005-2010, COM (2005) 177.

European Financial Management Association (EFMA) (2003), Annual Conference Paper No. 802, EFMA 2003 Helsinki Meetings.

European Parliament (2005), *Report on current state of integration of EU financial markets*, Committee on Economic and Monetary Affairs, Rapporteur: Ieke van den Burg, FINAL A6-0087/2005.

Eyerman, Edward and John Hatton (2004), "Association of British Insurers Call for Bond Market Standards" (www.gtnews.com).

Fan, Joseph, Sheridan Titman and Garry Twite (2004), "An International Comparison of Capital Structure and Debt Maturity Choices", unpublished paper presented at the 2003 European Finance Association Conference, forthcoming, *Journal of Finance*.

Fernandez, Frank (1999), *Liquidity Risk: New Approaches to Measurement and Monitoring*, Securities Industry Association, December.

Fink, Gerhard, Peter Haiss and Sirma Hristoforova (2003), *Bond Markets and Economic Growth*, IEF Working Papers, Research Institute for European Affairs, No. 49, Vienna, April.

Firth, M. (1995), "The Impact of Institutional Stockholders and Managerial Interests on the Capital Structure of Firms", *Managerial and Decision Economics*, Vol. 16, pp. 167-175.

Fleming, Michael (2001), *Measuring Treasury Market Liquidity*, Federal Reserve Bank of New York Staff Report 133, New York.

Furfine, Craig (2001), "Do Macro Announcements Still Move the Bond Market?", BIS *Quarterly Review*, June.

Furfine, C. and E.M. Remolona (2002), "Price discovery in a market under stress: The US Treasury market in fall 1998", BIS *Quarterly Review*.

Goldfinger, Charles (2003), *ISD II Directive Debate about the Trading Venue Diversity: The Tree and the Forest*, study by Global Electronic Finance Management, Brussels.

Golub, Ben and Leo Tilman (2000), "New Benchmarks for Debt Markets: No Room for Nostalgia in Fixed Income", Commentary, *Risk Magazine*, July.

Gravelle, Toni (2002), *The Microstructure of Multiple-Dealer Equity and Government Securities Markets: How They Differ*, Bank of Canada Working Paper 2002-9, Ottawa.

Green, Richard C., Burton Hollifield and Norman Schurhoff (2004), *Financial Intermediation and the Costs of Trading in an Opaque Market*, Carnegie Mellon Working Paper, Carnegie Mellon University, Tepper School of Business, GSIA Working Papers, No. 2004-11.

Hakansson, Nils (1998), *The Role of a Corporate Bond Market in an Economy – and in Avoiding Crises*, University of California Berkeley Working Paper, Berkeley, CA.

Hatton, John (2005), "European Bond Documentation and Ineffective Negative Pledges", *Fitch Ratings*, January.

Herring, Richard and Nathporn Chatusripitak (2001), *The Case of the Missing Market: The Bond Market and Why It Matters for Financial Development*, Wharton School working paper, Wharton School Center for Financial Institutions, University of Pennsylvania, Center for Financial Institutions Working Papers, No. 01-08.

Houweling, Patrick, Albert Mentink and Tim Vorst (2003), "How to Measure Corporate Bond Liquidity?", unpublished paper, Erasmus University, Rotterdam.

IFR Magazine (2005), 8 January.

IMF (2001), *International Capital Markets*, International Monetary Fund, Washington, D.C.

IMF (2004), *IMF Country Report No. 04/249*, Article IV Consultation Report, International Monetary Fund, Washington, D.C., August.

IMF and World Bank (2001), *Developing Government Bond Markets: A Handbook*, Washington, D.C.

International Financial Services London (2004), *International Financial Markets in the UK*, May

IOSCO (International Organisation of Securities' Commissions) (2001), *Transparency and Market Fragmentation*, report from the Technical Committee of the IOSCO, November.

ISMA (2004), *European Repo Market Survey*, December.

Issing, Otmar (2002), "Monetary Policy in an Environment of Global Financial Markets", paper presented at Launching Workshop of the ECB-CFS Research Network on Capital Markets and Financial Integration in Europe, Frankfurt am Main, 29 April.

Jeanneau, Serge (2000), "Derivatives Markets", BIS *Quarterly Review*, February.

Jones, Charles and Mark Lipson (1998), *Sixteenths: Direct Evidence on Institutional Trading Costs*, Columbia University Working Paper, New York, NY.

Joys, Jonathan (2001), *Electronic Trading Systems and Fixed Income Markets*, Working Paper, Centre for Digital Strategies, Tuck School of Business, Dartmouth University, Dartmouth, NH.

Karpoff (2004), Walt Disney Company's Sleeping Beauty Bonds – Duration Analysis, University of Washington School of Business Case Study, April (http://faculty.washington.edu/karpoff/FIN%20509/Sleeping_Beauty_case.doc).

Langton, John (2005), "Foreword", 2005 *Euromoney International Debt Capital Markets Handbook*, London: Euromoney Books.

Levich, Richard (1998), *International Financial Markets: Prices and Policies*, New York, NY: McGraw-Hill/Irwin.

Levin, Mattias (2003), *Competition, Fragmentation and Transparency: Providing the Regulatory Framework for Fair, Efficient and Dynamic European Securities Markets, Assessing the ISD Review*, CEPS Task Force Report No. 46, Centre for European Policy Studies, Brussels.

Levine, Ross (2004), *Finance and Growth: Theory and Evidence*, NBER Working Paper No. W10766, National Bureau of Economic Research, Cambridge, MA.

Levine, Ross and Sara Zervos (1999), *Stock Markets, Banks, and Economic Growth*, Policy Research Working Paper Series 1690, World Bank, Washington, D.C.

Levine, Ross, Thorsten Beck and Norman Loayza (1999), *Finance and the Sources of Growth*, Policy Research Working Paper Series 2057, World Bank, Washington, D.C.

Llewellyn, David (1999), *The Economic Rationale for Financial Regulation*, Occasional Paper 1, Financial Services Authority, London, April.

Manaster, Steven and Steven Man (1999), *Sources of Market-making Profits: Man Does Not Live by Spread Alone*, Virginia Tech Working Paper, Blacksburg, VA.

McCauley, Robert (1999), *The Euro and the Liquidity of European Fixed Income Markets*, BIS Committee on the Global Financial System (CGFS) Paper Series 11, Bank for International Settlements, Basel.

Melnik, Arie and Doron Nissim (2004), *Issue Costs in the Eurobond Market: The Effects of Market Integration*, Columbia University Working Paper, New York, NY.

MTS (2003), The Liquidity Pact: Enhancing Efficiency in the European Bond Market (www.mtsgroup.org/newcontent/news/d_new/ the_liquidity_pact_mts.pdf).

Munter, Päivi (2005), "ESpeed increases offer for MTS", *Financial Times*, 15 June.

Murinde, Victor, Juda Agung and Andy Mullineux (2004), "Patterns of Corporate Financing and Financial System Convergence in Europe", *Review of International Economics*, Vol. 12, No. 4, pp. 693-705, September.

OECD (Organisation for Economic Cooperation and Development) (2004), *Financial Market Trends*, October.

O'Hara, Maureen (1995), *Market Microstructure Theory*, Cambridge: Blackwell Business.

———— (2004), *Liquidity and Financial Market Stability*, National Bank of Belgium Working Paper No. 55, Brussels.

O'Kane, Gerry (2005), "Genesis of a European Revolution", *FT Mandate*, January.

Pagano, Marco and Ernst-Ludwig von Thadden (2004), "The European Bond Markets under EMU", *Oxford Review of Economy Policy*, Vol. 20 (4), pp. 531-554.

Persaud, Avinash (2000), "The Puzzling Decline in Financial Market Liquidity", *Risk Magazine*, June.

Pesek, William, Jr. (2005), "Bondholders in Japan Can Breathe Easily This Year", *International Herald Tribune*, 17 February.

Pierron, Axel (2004), *Electronic Trading in European Fixed Income Markets*, Celent Communications, http://www.celent.com/PressReleases/20041006/ETradingEuropean.htm.

Pirrong, Craig (2003), "Bund for Glory, or It's a Long Way to Tip a Market," University of Houston Working Paper, Houston, TX.

Rajan, Raghuram and Luigi Zingales (2002), "Banks and Markets: The Changing Character of European Finance", paper presented at Second ECB Central Banking Conference, Frankfurt am Main, 24-25 October.

Ready, Mark (2001), "The Specialist's Discretion: Stopped Orders and Price Improvement", *The Review of Financial Studies*, Vol. 14, No. 3, Fall, pp. 681-704.

Richebächer, Kurt (1969), "The Problems and Prospects of Integrating European Capital Markets", *Journal of Money, Credit and Banking*, Vol. 1, No. 3, August, pp. 336-346.

Ruth, Heather (1999), "The Future Is Now: What Should that Mean for Regulation of the Bond Markets?", speech delivered at the symposium on Reexamining the Regulation of Capital Markets for Debt Securities, Washington, D.C.

Saunders, Anthony, Anand Srinivasan and Ingo Walter (2002), "Price Formation in the OTC Corporate Bond Markets: A Field Study of the Inter-Dealer Market", *Journal of Economics and Business*, Vol. 54, No. 1, pp. 95-113.

Scalia, Antonio and Vlerio Vaca (1997), "Does Market Transparency Matter?", BIS Papers No. 2: *Market liquidity: Proceedings of a workshop*, Bank for International Settlements, Basel, April.

Schiantarelli, Fabio and Alessandro Sembenelli (1997), *The Maturity Structure of Debt: Determinants and Effects on Firms' Performance*, World

Bank Policy Research Working Paper WPS1699, World Bank, Washington, D.C.

Schultz, Paul (2000), "Corporate Bond Trading Costs: A Peek Behind the Curtain", *Journal of Finance*, Vol. 56, No. 2, pp. 677-698.

Shen, Qian, Andrew Szakmary and Subhash Sharma (2004), "Price Momentum and Trading Volume in Commodity Futures Markets", paper presented at Financial Management Association Meetings, New Orleans, LA, October.

Shulman, Doug (2004), "An Overview of the Regulation of Bond Markets", testimony before the Committee on Banking, Housing and Urban Affairs, United States Senate, 17 June.

Simensen, Ivar (2005a), "Demand prompts Athens to beef up 30-year offer", *Financial Times*, 3 March.

———— (2005b), "50-year bond issue for telecom Italia", *Financial Times*, 8 March.

Solans, Eugenio Domingo (2003), Member of the Governing Council and of the Executive Board of the European Central Bank, speech delivered at the 7th Central European Covered Bond Conference, Berlin, 13 October.

Standard and Poor's (2005), *Annual European Corporate Default Study and Rating Transitions*, Global Fixed Income Research, May.

The Bond Market Association (TBMA) (2004), *eCommerce in the Fixed Income Markets*, the 2004 review of electronic transaction systems.

———— (2005a), *European Bond Pricing Sources and Services: Implications for Price Transparency in the European Bond Market*, April.

———— (2005b), "European Bond Markets", presentation to the European Securities Committee, Brussels, 13 July.

Unger, Laura (2001), Testimony concerning the Effects of Decimalization on the Securities Markets before the Subcommittee on Securities and Investment, Committee on Banking, Housing, and Urban Affairs, United States Senate, 24 May.

Verband deutscher Hypothekenbanken (VDH) (2004), The Pfandbrief: *Europe's Biggest Bond Market*.

Wahrenburg, Mark (2001), *Trading System Competition and Market-Maker Competition*, BIS Papers No. 7, Bank for International Settlements, Basel.

Wallenstein, Stephen (2000), "Beyond Bond Markets 2000: The Electronic Frontier and Regulation of the Capital Markets for Debt Securities", *Law and Contemporary Problems*, Vol. 63, Summer.

Welteke, Ernst (2000), *Different Aspects of Change in Today's Financial Systems*, BIS Review 80/2000, Bank for International Settlements, Basel.

Wolswijk, Guido and Jakob de Haan (2005), *Government Debt Management in the Euro Area*, ECB Occasional Paper Series No. 25, European Central Bank, Frankfurt, March.

Annex I

EU Legislation Governing the Securities Market

- **Stock exchange admission.** Council Directive of 79/279/EEC coordinating the conditions for the admission of securities to official stock exchange listing, OJ L 66 of 16.3.1979.

- **Stock exchange listing particulars.** Council Directive 87/345 of 22 June 1987 amending Directive 80/390 co-ordinating the requirement for the drawing-up, scrutiny, and distribution of the listing particulars to be published for the admission of securities to official stock exchange listing, OJ L 185 of 4.7.1987; Eurolist amendments, Directive 94/18/EC, OJ L 135 of 31.5.1994.

- **Mutual recognition of public-offer prospectuses.** Council Directive 90/211 of 23 April 1990 amending directive 80/390 in respect of the mutual recognition of public-offer prospectuses as stock exchange listing particulars, OJ L 112 of 3.5.1990.

- **Prospectuses.** Council Directive 89/298 co-ordinating the requirements for the drawing-up, scrutiny and distribution for the prospectus to be published when securities are offered to the public, OJ L 124 of 5.5.1989.

- **Codified listing admission.** Directive 2001/34/EC of the European Parliament and of the Council of 28 May 2001 on the admission of securities to official stock exchange listing and on the information to be published on those securities, OJ L 184 of 6.7.2001 (codifies the provisions of all the directives listed before).

- **Insider trading.** Council Directive 89/592 coordinating regulations on insider dealing, OJ L 334 of 18.11.1989.

- **Investment services.** Council Directive 93/6 of 10 May 1993 on investment services in the securities field, OJ L 141 of 11 June 1993.

- **Periodic disclosure.** Council Directive 82/121 on information to be published on a regular basis by companies the shares of which have been admitted to official stock exchange listing, OJ L 48 of 20.02.82.

- **Publication of information on major holdings.** Council Directive 88/627 on the information to be published when a major holding in a listed company is acquired or disposed of, OJ L 348 of 17.12.1988.

FSAP Directives

- **Prospectus.** Directive 2003/71/EC on the prospectus to be published when securities are offered to the public or admitted to trading and amending directive 2001/34, adopted by the Council on 15 July 2003, OJ L 345 of 31.12.2003; implementing measures in Commission regulation (EC) No 809/2004 of 29 April 2004, OJ L 149 of 30.4.2004.
- **Market abuse.** Directive 2003/6/EC on insider dealing and market manipulation, OJ L 096 of 12.4.2003.
- **Transparency.** Directive 2004/109/EC of the European Parliament and of the Council on the harmonisation of transparency requirements with regard to information about issuers whose securities are admitted to trading on a regulated market and amending directive 2001/34, OJ L 390 of 31.12.2004.
- **Markets in Financial Instruments.** Directive 2004/39/EC of the European Parliament and the Council on investment services and regulated markets, and amending Council directives 85/611/EEC and European Parliament and Council Directive 2000/12/EC, OJ L 145/1 of 21.4.2004.

Financial Reporting Directives

- **Fourth Company Law Directive (78/660).** public and private limited companies; presentation and content of annual report and accounts, valuation rules and disclosure, OJ L 222 of 14.8.1978; amended on 8 November 1990, OJ L 317 of 16.11.1990
- **Seventh Company Law Directive (83/349).** consolidated accounts of public or private limited companies, OJ L 193 of 18.7.1983; amended on 8 November 1990, OJ L 317 of 16.11.1990
- **International Accounting Standards (IAS).** Regulation (EC)1606/2002 on the application of IAS for listed companies in the EU, OJ L 243 of 11.9.2002.